INTRODUCTION TO PATENTS INFORMATION

Fourth edition

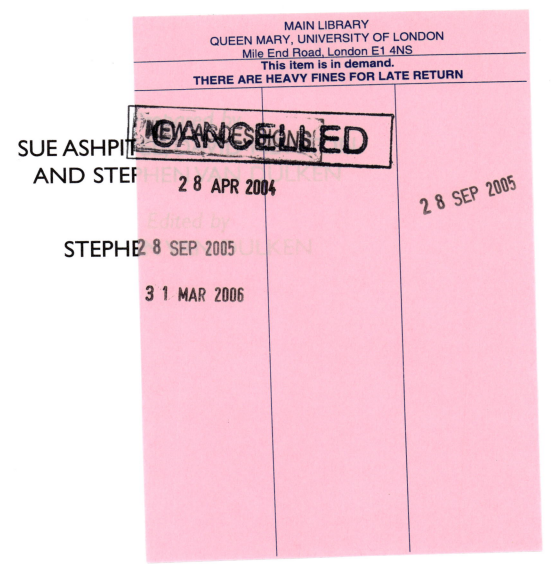

SUE ASHPITEL
AND STEPHEN VAN DULKEN

Edited by

STEPHEN VAN DULKEN

THE BRITISH LIBRARY

Introduction to patents information
ISBN 0 7123 0862 8

Published by:

The British Library
96 Euston Road
London NW1 2DB

First edition 1990
Second edition 1992
Third edition 1998
Fourth edition 2002

British Library Cataloguing in Publication Data
A CIP record is available from The British Library

Desktop publishing by Concerto, Leighton Buzzard, Bedfordshire. Tel: 01525 378757

Printed in Great Britain by Atheneum Press Ltd, Gateshead, Tyne and Wear

CONTENTS

LIST OF FIGURES iv

PREFACE TO THE FOURTH EDITION v

1. THE BASICS OF PATENT INFORMATION 1

2. THE PATENT COOPERATION TREATY 12

3. THE EUROPEAN PATENT CONVENTION 19

4. THE BRITISH PATENT SYSTEM .32

5. THE UNITED STATES PATENT SYSTEM 49

6. THE GERMAN PATENT SYSTEM 61

7. THE JAPANESE PATENT SYSTEM 71

8. PATENT CLASSIFICATION 85

9. FINDING AND USING PATENT INFORMATION 92

10. WHERE TO SEARCH FOR PATENT INFORMATION IN THE UK . 99

APPENDIX: ONLINE RESOURCES 105

BIBLIOGRAPHY 111

GLOSSARY OF PATENT TERMS 124

INID AND COUNTRY CODES 127

INDEX 135

LIST OF FIGURES

2.1   Procedure for applying under the Patent Cooperation Treaty 14

2.2   Front page of a PCT application from the Coca-Cola Company 16

3.1   Procedure for applying for a European Patent .21

3.2   Application for a patent on a vacuum cleaner component 23

3.3   Front page of a European grant 25

3.4   European search report 26

4.1   Progress of a UK patent application under the Patents Act 1977 33

4.2   Front page of a British application 35

4.3   Front page of a British grant 36

4.4   Filed applications listed in the *Patents and Designs Journal* 39

4.5   Published applications listed by subject in the *Patents and Designs Journal* 41

4.6   Published applications listed by name in the *Patents and Designs Journal* 42

4.7   British status data from the official database .47

5.1   Front page of an American application 52

5.2   Front page, description and claims of an American grant 53

6.1   Front page of a German application 66

6.2   Front page of a German grant 67

6.3   Front page of a German utility model 68

7.1   Front page of a Japanese application 75

7.2   Claims and beginning of description of a Japanese application 77

7.3   Front page of a Japanese grant 78

7.4   Front page of a Japanese utility model 79

7.5   English abstract of a Japanese application 80

7.6   Computer-generated translation of claims of a Japanese application 82

8.1   The International Patent Classification on the web at
        http://classifications.wipo.int/fulltext/new_ipc/index.htm 86

8.2   Annotated page from the 7th edition of the *International Patent Classification* 91

A.1   Bibliographic record from the **Esp@cenet** database 109

PREFACE TO THE FOURTH EDITION

The British Library (rather than the Patent Office) houses the United Kingdom's national collection of patents from around the world, with over 47 million patents from 40 countries or authorities. We offer at our St Pancras site in London many patent information services including online searching, publications and short free workshops on the use of patents as a source of information. A pass is needed to be admitted as a reader. Our patents home page on the web is **http://www.bl.uk/patents**.

The British Library originally published this guide as a coursebook for its workshops of the same name. These origins are reflected in a certain bias towards British interests, but patent documentation for the United States, Germany and Japan as well as the international systems all have their own chapters. The guide should be useful for patents users abroad as well as in Britain as a practical guide to how the patent system works for librarians and information scientists, rather than the lawyer. It is needed as the Internet can be a great boon but it is often not obvious how to search or how to interpret the results. The good response that we have received has led us to bring out subsequent editions.

The book is primarily for those who are either totally new to patents, or who have not yet fully mastered the basics of how to approach patents. At the same time, we hope that it will also be useful for those who are more advanced in their knowledge. It is, however, not legal advice and we are not responsible for any errors of omission and commission. Those who need legal advice should consult patent agents or the relevant patent office.

The book is divided into three main sections.

- The first (after a preliminary chapter) explains the main points of the patent documentation of six patent offices: Britain, the European Patent Convention, the Patent Cooperation Treaty patents, the United States, Germany and Japan.

- The second covers finding patent information (a new chapter), patent classification and patent information resources in the United Kingdom.

- The third consists of appendices. These cover online, compact disc and Internet sources, a bibliography, a glossary and lists of INID and country codes.

This fourth edition has been extensively revised, particularly reflecting changes in Japanese and American documentation and numerous new databases on the Internet. Many front pages from patent specifications have been used to show the source of much of the data that is actually searched on the web. The bibliography has also been revised. It is noticeable that each edition adds more detail partly because users' expectations rise, and partly because the more basic search tools become more difficult and complex. As web resources will inevitably change we suggest that patent users periodically revisit our home page as new and changed sites will be listed on our detailed lists of links.

Little attempt has been made to cover anything other than the current documentation as it is assumed that users will be mainly interested in recent patent materials. Older material is covered in detail on an authority by authority basis in our *International guide to official industrial property publications*.

Material for this edition was written by David Newton and Sue Ashpitel as well as by the editor, Stephen van Dulken. The publishing editor was Anthony Warshaw and the book was seen through the press by Paul Wilson.

Every effort was made to make this publication as accurate and up to date as possible, but the British Library cannot accept responsibility for any errors.

Suggestions for alterations or additions for future editions would be welcome. Send your suggestions to: Stephen van Dulken, Patents Information, The British Library, 96 Euston Road, London NW1 2DB, or via email to patents-information@bl.uk.

1. THE BASICS OF PATENT INFORMATION

Before looking at what patents are and how the patent system works, we need to put
them in the context of intellectual property as a whole, which is quite literally about the
property of the intellect: things that we create by our minds. What follows gives a general
picture and is biased towards British practice. It does not provide for all exceptions and is
certainly not legal advice. The intellectual-property.gov website at
http://www.intellectual-property.gov.uk/std/faq/how_protect/index.htm is
useful for explaining how many concepts can be protected under British law.

The main concepts in intellectual property

Patents, trade marks and designs constitute **industrial property** although it is now more
common to talk about **intellectual property**, which is these concepts plus copyright
and, in practice, other aspects. Rights in intellectual property can be bought, sold, licensed
or inherited just like real estate. Similarly, litigation can occur. Unregistered rights are
literally that and are not listed, published or indexed by any official body. Registered rights
at the patent office are applied for at each national office where protection is sought for
that country. Inventors and designers should not think "How can I patent my idea?" or
"Which is the patent number for that person's idea?" but rather "How is that idea
protected under the intellectual propery system?" That is because several aspects can be
used to protect the idea.

Copyright is about original literary, dramatic, musical or artistic works. In inventions it
would apply to the exact wording of instructions for use. It is quite literally a right against
deliberate copying, hence the name. A defence that you are unaware of the other person's
work, and that you independently created a similar work, will be good. In the UK as in
most countries (but not in the USA) copyright is automatic and unregistered. The Patent
Office suggests that those wanting to take advantage of it should send the material to
themselves by registered post and then keep it opened as evidence of when it was thought
of. It is also a good idea to state e.g. "Copyright XYZ Company 2002". The © symbol
can be used instead of "copyright". In Europe and the USA copyright lasts for the author's
life plus 70 years.

Registered designs are for the distinctive appearance of a manufactured article. This can
cover anything from toys to shoes or clothes. They are registered at the Patent Office for a
term of up to 25 years (in 5 year portions paid for by fees). Violation of such rights lead to
infringement cases. Registered designs can be for items that would be automatically
protected by copyright but provide stronger protection as deliberate copying does not
have to be shown. Relevant databases are listed by the British Library at
http://www.bl.uk/services/information/patents/deslinks.html.

Design right is a uniquely British form of protection which was introduced by 1988
legislation. It provides protection to the original outward appearance of manufactured
articles. It can be for part of an article unlike registered designs. It does not provide

protection where one article must fit or match another as in car doors fitting in with the general line of the car. It is not registered and lasts for 10 years from the first marketing of the product or for a maximum of 15 years.

Trade marks (or in the USA trademarks and in Canada trade-marks) distinguish one trader's goods or services from those of another. It covers words and devices (drawings or logos etc.) or combinations of them and since 1994 has also covered shapes (such as the familiar Coca Cola bottle), smells and sounds. Protection is given in Britain (but not in Europe) to trade names that are not registered at a patent office provided that adequate proof is supplied that the name is known. Registration at the patent office is for named, specific goods or services within 34 classes of goods and 11 of services. Trade marks must be distinctive and must not be deceptive or conflict with other marks. Trade marks can be similar provided that they are in different classes and do not confuse consumers (sometimes marks in different classes will confuse). Trade marks last forever provided that they continue to be used, renewal fees are paid every 10 years and are kept distinctive as a trade mark (are capitalised or otherwise made obviously different from other material). In the USA you are also required to use ® after the mark to indicate that it has been registered or ™ if it is pending registration or is unregistered. This is not required in the UK but is considered good practice. Relevant databases are listed by the British Library at **http://www.bl.uk/services/information/patents/tmlinks.html**.

To remember the above it is helpful to think of an idea and to see how it might be protected. Many business ideas to, say, promote the sale of petrol are not patentable but the above concepts may apply. There are other, less used forms (at least for inventions) which are allied to these but this book will concentrate on the final form, patents.

What is a patent?

A patent is a contract between the state and the applicant by which a temporary monopoly is granted in return for disclosing all details of the invention. This is a simplification: what happens is not that the applicant is given a monopoly but rather that no one else can exploit that invention. This is because a patent may be useless except when combined with another, possibly patented, idea. It is often difficult to distinguish what is in theory patentable from other areas. Patents normally involve a practical advantage in a product (or in the method of making a known product) to make it more effective, making it cheaper to manufacture or providing an alternative product. Few patents are for totally new ideas although this is of course possible. All these involve advantages for the producer and/or consumer. They can be remembered as BCD: "better, cheaper, different". Chemistry and biology are in fact making it more difficult to fit inventions into such a framework which was originally meant for mechanical engineering.

Criteria for the grant of patents

The word "patent" is often used to describe any patent document. It is more correct if used only for a document to which rights are, or have been, given. "Specification" or "patent specification" can be used to describe any document describing an invention which is going, or has gone, through the patent system. It does not imply that the idea is or was necessarily new or accepted as valid.

All patent rights must be applied for at a patent office to gain rights in that country or regional patent system. Such applications are made by submitting a specification in the language(s) acceptable to that patent office.

In order for a patent application to become a valid patent it must meet several criteria:

It must be novel. **Novelty** means that it must be original as a patent, and indeed new in any published format. **Prior art** is the phrase used for earlier material that could invalidate it and extends across the world. In addition, the application is unlikely to be accepted if the applicant describes it (except in confidence), or if it is manufactured before the application is submitted, so it is vital that it is kept secret until this time. Otherwise the invention is open to anyone to manufacture it. Only the USA keeps to "first to invent" (which must be proven) rather than "first to file".

It must not be obvious. This means that it must not be a predictable improvement of something already in existence or described in the published literature. Theoretically if an uninventive person who knows all prior art thinks that an idea is an inventive step, then it is not **obvious.**

It must be useful. It must do or be something of practical benefit, rather than being a scientific observation, or a work of art. Briefly it must be better, different or cheaper than existing products: all are practicable benefits to the producer and/or consumer.

It must be capable of being industrially reproduced. This criterion is applied very loosely: many chemical patents, for instance, refer to substances that cannot be reproduced in a factory environment.

It must not be illegal or immoral. Examples of illegal patents would be land mines, which have been banned in Britain since Princess Diana's campaign. In the 1930s patents for contraceptives were not allowed in Britain. However, some countries allow "illegal" patents if the applicant intends only to export the product to countries where they are legal.

It must give full details of how the invention works. The patent must be detailed enough so that someone skilled in the art can reconstruct the invention from the description and drawings alone. This is fundamental, and failure to give sufficient detail can be cause to refuse a patent. An exception is made for microorganism patents where a sample must be kept at a recognised depository, and increasingly now for gene sequence specifications where the actual sequences may be stored on a CD-ROM or other medium at the patent office.

Some categories of invention are generally considered unpatentable. Increasingly these categories have become fewer as computer software, algorithms, microorganisms and gene sequences have increasingly been accepted as patentable in many countries after pressure from industry for stronger protection. Even medical treatments such as keyhole surgery have been suggested. Generally speaking the USA has led the way in allowing such patents, and the European Patent Office has (usually) followed. The member states of the European Patent Convention have then done the same for their national patents. Britain has rejected the idea of "business method" patents which Japan and the USA have accepted. Local patent agents or the local patent office should be consulted if there is any doubt if an idea is patentable in that jurisdiction.

The Budapest Treaty for the International Recognition of the Deposit of Microorganisms for the Purposes of Patent Procedure, which dates back to 1977, is used for patents where a microorganism sample must be used in order to understand the invention. INID code (83) on the front page of such a patent specification records the site and deposit number of the microorganism at a recognised depository.

Basic patenting procedure

The basic procedure of applying for patents is regulated by the Paris Convention for the Protection of Industrial Property of 1883, to which most countries belong.

An applicant for a patent draws up, usually with the help of a patent agent, a **patent specification**. This consists of a description, drawings, and the claims to the monopoly requested although some authorities allow less detail to be initially filed. This specification, together with the relevant forms and fees if required, is filed at (normally) the applicant's national patent office. The material sent in distinguishes between the applicant, the person(s) and/or corporate entity that intends to "work" the invention and which owns the rights, and the inventors who actually designed the invention. Sometimes the inventors are the applicants. It is wrong to call such a specification a "patent" document unless it has actually been granted protection (as it implies rights that have not yet been granted and which may never be granted). Before filing the invention should be kept secret (unless disclosed in confidence or to those providing professional assistance such as patent agents).

This initial, "**priority**" **application** for a patent is in a sense provisional evidence of novelty. This is because the invention may turn out not to be new, or only an obvious improvement. Provided it is acceptable it is this filing date which is used to establish which of two rival patent applications is the first, or to establish that the applicant does have a claim to a monopoly right. This extends across the world so that a filing in, say, China on 1 June would "anticipate" a filing in Britain on 2 June even if neither party intended to patent the invention in the other country. Provided someone noticed, the British application would be unsuccessful. The United States is the only country which recognises "**first to invent**" rather than "**first to file**". The latter is much easier to prove if conflict arises.

A filing or application number is also given to the application at this stage and there may be a "**preliminary examination**", which is a rough check to ensure that e.g. the drawings are clear and that fees have been paid. The filing number is also the priority number which can be used to claim priority when making subsequent filings of the same invention in other patent offices. Most countries print the priority country (usually as a two-letter country code), date and filing number on their patent documents. This data can also be used to identify other members of the "patent family" as different patent offices publish "equivalents" of the original invention.

Should the applicant want foreign protection outside the home country this must be applied for separately for each country. Under the Paris Convention these applications must be made within 12 months of the priority date. Most applicants wait the full 12 months until they actually file abroad as this helps in planning strategy. As the patent term nowadays nearly always dates from the application in the foreign patent office this also maximises the length of the term. This priority information can be used by citizens or

Mile End Library

Christmas Vacation 17th Dec - 9th Jan
Extended Vacation Loans
Ordinary Loans borrowed or renewed
from Saturday 19th Nov
will be due back on Friday 13th Jan
One Week Loans borrowed or renewed
from Saturday 10th Dec
will be due back on Wednesday 11th Jan
One Day Loans borrowed on
Friday 16th December
will be due back on Monday 9th Jan

Borrowed Items 24/11/2016 11:25
XXXXXX5629

Item Title	Due Date
* Introduction to patents information	01/12/2016
Writing up your university assignments and research projects : a practical handbook	13/01/2017

* Indicates items borrowed today
PLEASE NOTE
If you still have overdue books on loan
you may have more fines to pay

residents of any country belonging to the 1883 Paris Convention for the Protection of Industrial Property, or, since 1 January 1996, from countries belonging to the World Trade Organization (WTO). Such filings, if published, are called **equivalents** and together they form the **patent family**.

Some companies wait until almost the initial publication of the specification before filing abroad. This is called "filing outside the Convention" and is liable to mean that the priority document will itself be used as evidence that the application is not new.

In some countries, the applicant may be asked some time after filing the specification for a fee so that a search for anything that suggests that the invention is not new, or is only obvious, can be carried out. Other countries wait for the specification to be published before doing so, while other, usually smaller countries do not carry out a search at all.

Many industrialised countries publish applications 18 months after the priority (not filing) date. This means that the equivalents in the patent family tend to appear within a few weeks of each other. In practice, the growing popularity of the Patent Cooperation Treaty (PCT) scheme has meant that there are often only two publications at 18 months: that in the original country and the equivalent PCT specification, which serves as a basis for later securing protection in countries designated in it. The situation can get more complicated. A British applicant who intends to ask for protection in much of the world can legitimately make a priority filing in Britain; file in the PCT at 12 months; drop the British application; and the PCT specification is published at 18 months in which protection is requested for Britain and other countries through the regional European Patent Convention. This is not unethical and is in fact a sensible way both to cut and to delay costs while the market for the product, and its novelty, are assessed. Publication of the application does not imply that the patent office thinks that the invention is new. Its purpose is to allow others to note the existence of this invention, which they might infringe if rights are later given to it.

A number is given to the published application, which is normally different from the filing number (Germany is an exception). A **document code** typically follows the number. This code is normally an A for applications and a number may follow the letter. A1 is typical. Ideally the published specifications are cited as e.g. GB 2331024 A. GB indicates the country, 2331024 is the number assigned at publication, and A is the document code showing that it was an application. The code B is normally used for the second stage grants. In some cases a number besides 1 will be used as a suffix, hence say A3 or B8. These numbers often have significance in identifying the exact document as different codes may be used for different documents relating to the same invention and which have the same number. Failure to use these elements correctly may mean getting the wrong document. Increasingly these codes are becoming standardised as recommended in the WIPO standard 16 at **http://www.wipo.int/scit/en/standards/pdf/st_16.pdf**.

Each patent office individually decides without consulting other offices whether or not to grant a patent. The bigger offices will do this by carrying out a **substantive examination**. This is based on considering the claims, even if additional novel information is in the description. Such additional matter would be ignored if not in the claims. On the other hand, the additional novel information could be used to show that the claims of another patent application were not novel as they had already been disclosed. If a patent document that the applicant could not be aware of is taken into consideration (such as a rival application filed the day before) then novelty, but not obviousness, is taken into account. A "mosaic" of documents which together suggests that an idea has been done before is not acceptable as valid prior art unless the documents referred to each other so that such references could be easily followed up. References from books, articles and conference proceedings that dated from before the priority date can also be used to invalidate some or all of the application, as well as something seen in public.

Some offices, mostly smaller, merely register applications without checking for novelty. Others do check but will grant the patent if the applicant insists (e.g. France and Belgium). Examples of countries that do examine in detail and reject or modify those that they do not regard as new are Britain, the United States, Germany and the regional European Patent Office. A patent application that has been examined for novelty is said to be a "strong" patent as if it had been done before this is likely to have been spotted. If the application has not been checked by a patent office then it is often called a "weak" patent.

If an application is considered acceptable then it is published a second time, usually in modified form, as a **granted patent**. The number given to it is often the same as that on the published application (the USA and Japan are exceptions). The document code is typically B1 (Germany is an exception where it will be C1 or C2 and in the USA it may be B2). Several years have usually elapsed since the priority application. Some countries have an **opposition period** during which the patent can be opposed on the grounds of non-novelty by interested parties. Germany is an example. Others, like Britain, allow others to claim the patent is invalid and to instigate proceedings against it at any time during the patent term. A successful attack on the patent would mean its **revocation** as if it were never protected at all. These procedures occur independently in each country. It is now that the person or corporate entity owning the patent can take those **infringing** the patent to court as a civil action and hence prevent them from using the idea, and hopefully obtain remedies or damages as financial compensation.

In most countries it is necessary to pay, at intervals (often annual), **renewal fees** or (in the USA) maintenance fees to the Patent Office to keep the patent in force. Otherwise the patent **lapses** from protection. Failure to pay the fees means that the invention is open to anyone else to manufacture or import the invention in that country.

Otherwise the patent runs its term and "**expires**". The full **term of protection** used to vary from country to country but 20 years from the earliest date of filing in that country (not the priority date) is now almost universal. This is because of the Agreement on Trade-Related Aspects of Intellectual Property (TRIPs) to which countries wishing to join the World Trade Organization, the successor body to GATT, must adhere. It provided for minimum 20 year terms from filing in that country which in fact has been adopted as the exact terms worldwide. Developing countries were however allowed until the years 2005 or 2006 to comply with the provisions, which also include allowing patents for pharmaceutical products and processes.

An exception in the length of the terms is increasingly being made for pharmaceuticals through what are called (in Europe) **Supplementary Protection Certificates** (SPCs) which are issued on request by the patent office involved. In other regions they can have other names such as patent extensions. Plant protection products such as fertilizers and pesticides are sometimes also protected in this way. The grounds are that in such cases the owners have not been able to exploit the inventions as they had to wait for permission by regulatory authorities to market them. The SPC effectively adds the lost period of time onto the end of the term.

A patent cannot be re-registered after expiry.

Some patent offices publish specifications for **utility models**. These are specifications where a smaller inventive step is required than for patents, often only for mechanical or electrical inventions. The name for such specifications vary, such as "petty patents", "short-term" patents or (in German) *Gebrauchsmustern*. The term of protection is usually shorter than for patents, typically being for six or ten years, and there is no examination for novelty. Germany, Japan and France are the principal countries which publish utility models. The European Union is planning to bring about a European utility model which would be a registration scheme (with no examination for novelty) run from the Office for the Harmonisation of the Internal Market (OHIM) at Alicante, Spain.

Some people prefer not to obtain a patent and wish to disclose the idea for all to use. This could be because of a kind and charitable nature but is normally because they do not think that it is worth the effort of patenting while wishing to avoid someone else claiming a monopoly and demanding licensing fees. By deliberately publishing details of the idea in say a journal they make it part of the prior art and therefore not patentable. Only the USA officially publishes such **disclosures** through its patent system as "statutory inventions" (previously "defensives", a term that is often still used). The journal *Research Disclosures* publishes an abstract and drawing of such disclosures and is indexed online, and some companies publish their own disclosures on paper or on the Internet.

Layout of patents

The different parts of a patent specification are as follows. It is based on typical layouts in patent specifications since about the late 1970s. Those before then are likely to lack a front page and search reports. Many aspects, especially in the front pages, relate to standards written (after consultation) by the World Intellectual Property Organization (WIPO). Details of their standards are at **http://www.wipo.int/scit/en/standards/standards. htm**.

Front page. In the same way that a book will have a title page, patents have a front page which gives useful bibliographical details. An abstract (compiled nowadays by the applicant) and, if appropriate, a representative illustration, structural formula or circuit diagram is usually given as well. Although this layout is becoming increasingly standardised the information given can vary from country to country, as can be seen by comparing the information in the front pages of different patent system's patent documents in this book. The use of two-letter country codes and INID codes to identify pieces of information has been widely adopted, especially for INID codes. This book gives the codes on pages 127–134.

Opening statement. This can vary but usually states the problem.

Background information. This is often interesting and American patents are particularly likely to have a discussion of the "state of the art" with references to key patents, books or journal articles.

Problem. The nature of the technical problem is often outlined.

Description of the invention. The description explains the inventive step and how it works, with numbered reference to illustrations. In the case of chemistry there are often "Examples" of specific structures within a wide-ranging Markush structure.

Claims. The numbered claims cover the legal aspects of the monopoly with the first being the main claim and the later, dependent claims referring back to earlier claims in describing what is new about the invention. Applicants like the claims to cover as much territory as possible but the examiner may force a modification of a claim if the area of monopoly seems unjustifiably large. In a published application the claims are merely an attempt to get protection while the grant has the claims that are recognised in law.

Illustrations (if relevant). There are as many as are required to show how the invention works.

Search report. This is usually on the front or last page, sometimes on the second page, of the specification. This can vary in its detail but will at a minimum consist of a list of patent or other documents suggesting that some at least of the invention is not new, or merely obvious. More detailed search reports would indicate which claims in the application were affected, the kind of relevance (mainly novelty or obviousness), and the exact page and line numbers thought to be relevant in the cited document. Some patent offices do not carry out searches, or do so and do not print them in the specification. Sometimes they are in the published applications and sometimes in the grant (as in the USA). Search reports can be valuable when trying to assess if the invention is truly new, and are also often used in "data mining" to try to establish if, say, one technology is more dependent on older sources than another.

There are differences in how the specifications are laid out. Line numbering within the description and claims are normal, and pages are usually numbered. However, electronic formats may result in a different page 9 for the same specification, and so there has been talk of assigning paragraph numbers within the description. The European Patent Office now has paragraph numbers within each specification. The order in which the illustrations or search report are placed can vary from country to country. The main countries to place the illustrations before the description are Britain and the USA while the illustrations follow the description in the European Patent Office, France, Germany, Japan and the Patent Cooperation Treaty. Search reports are generally at the back (Britain, Patent Cooperation Treaty, European Patent Office and now France) or on the front (USA, Germany, Japan). The USA and Japan put their search reports on the grants while Germany may have them on either stage. Japan is unusual in placing its numbered claims before rather than after the description. The length of the patent specification will vary widely but 20 to 30 pages is typical. They can be hundreds of pages long if necessary.

There has also been standardisation in classification. Nearly all countries now use the International Patent Classification (IPC) on their patent specifications, although Britain and the USA also use national classifications. This helps subject searching on an international basis using online searching.

The advantages of patents

There are many benefits in using the million patent documents published annually as a source of information. They mainly relate to technical information, but commercial information from patents can also be useful.

Currency of data. The publication of a patent application is often the first time that the information has ever been published. The details of an invention have to be kept secret before an application is submitted to the Patent Office. Since the 1970s most industrialised countries publish the application 18 months after the original filing on which it is based. This may seem like a long time but the above still tends to hold true.

Uniquely available information. It has been estimated that 85% of the information in patents is never published anywhere else. This is probably less true of those in the fields of biology and chemistry.

Full and practical descriptions. A patent specification must have sufficient detail in text and illustrations so that an expert in the same branch of industry can recreate the invention.

Ease of comparison. Patents have become increasingly standardised in their layout, although there are exceptions. This is useful since it saves the time of anyone who needs to look at numerous patents, or who is looking at foreign language patents. This is especially true of the front page.

Availability of translations. An application must be made in every country in which protection is required. As every country publishes in its own language(s), this means that there may be many English language specifications which are in effect translations of the technical content of foreign language patents.

Supplementary information. Many patents are published with search reports prepared by the patent offices, listing patents and any other literature which were found in the literature search on the subject matter of the invention. This may be interesting in itself, and can be important in trying to determine if a published application is likely to succeed.

Commercial information. Statistical analysis is often for business reasons. Caution should be used especially by those not familiar with patents. Generally speaking, it is awkward to compare patenting trends between countries in their own systems as fees and requirements may vary, making comparisons meaningless. Regional patenting systems such as the European Patent Convention may mean that national systems are largely ignored in their favour. Therefore it is normal to use the Patent Cooperation Treaty, European Patent Convention or the American system to compare patenting trends.

Copyright. No patents are covered by copyright so you can freely copy as much as you want of patent documents, and indeed experiment by making prototypes from them. What you may not be able to do is to make or import them.

The uses of patents

By examining the advantages we can see a number of possible uses for patents information:

Current awareness. Since patents are often the first or even the only source of information on a technological advance they are an essential element of any current awareness effort.

Avoiding infringement. The patent literature on any topic where manufacturing or importing is contemplated should be studied to avoid infringing patents that are currently protected in particular jurisdictions.

Inspiration. Browsing through the patents on a subject of interest can encourage interesting ideas, particularly as it is often possible to find the same concepts being used in unrelated industries.

Licensing opportunities. Even if a patent is still protected in the country it may be possible to negotiate a licence for its manufacture or import.

Preliminary stages in research and development. A search through the patents literature should always be done when beginning a research project to avoid wasteful duplication. The idea may be protected by a patent, or that patent may have passed out of protection, so that a detailed description is ready for use.

Information on competitors. Checking the current patent literature increases awareness of what competitors are doing, and this can be analysed.

Trends in technology. The patent classification can be used to plot technological trends by using a simple online search for later analysis.

Patent specifications and the gazettes and indexes associated with them are used by a broad cross section of the community. This includes inventors and companies, hoping to secure a temporary monopoly for a new idea; patent agents and searchers, carrying out infringement searches, to ensure that an apparently new idea is not blocked for use by a patent still in force; researchers generally, looking to see if an idea has ever been patented; the legal profession, gathering evidence for a court case involving patent rights; those looking for a solution to a technical problem; and anyone interested in what has been done in the past, or currently, in a particular topic. There is growing interest in analysis by financial, marketing and academic workers.

The novice in patents will inevitably be limited by inexperience in exploiting such possibilities. A lack of technical background, and of access to electronic databases, will also hamper and limit research. Paying an expert to carry out research on your behalf may be necessary.

Further reading

Challenging claims! Patenting computer programs in Europe and the USA. D. Attridge, *Intellectual Property Quarterly*, 2001, 1, 22-49.

Patent citation analysis: a closer look at the basic input data from patent search reports. B. Bettels and J. Michel, *Scientometrics*, 2001, 51 (1), 185-201.

European and UK software and business method patents are in a holding pattern. A. Laakkonen, *World Intellectual Property Report*, 2001, 15 (7), 28-31.

Intellectual property and the human genome. G. Laurie, *CIPA*, 2001, 30 (7), 352-354.

Fighting the patent wars. M Likhovski, *European Intellectual Property Review*, 2001, 23 (6), 267-274 [on business method patents].

The patentability of biological material: continuing contradiction and confusion. M. Llewellyn, *European Intellectual Property Review*, 2000, 22 (5), 191-197.

Patents for chemicals, pharmaceuticals and biotechnology: fundamentals of global law, practice and strategy. P.W. Grubb. Oxford: Clarendon Press, 1999.

2. THE PATENT COOPERATION TREATY

The Patent Cooperation Treaty (PCT) provides, on the basis of a single "international" application in one language, for an international search which will be effective in any of the countries which are party to the treaty. The PCT is administered by the World Intellectual Property Organization (WIPO) in Geneva. Most new major inventions are now published as PCT applications.

The first PCT applications were filed on 1 June 1978 and publication began in October 1978. The number of PCT applications is steadily increasing. In 2000 79,858 applications were published, an increase of 17% over 1999. Only 16,143 were published in 1990. Of the 90,948 filings in 2000 38,171, or 42.0%, were from the USA; 12,029 (13.2%) from Germany; 9,402 (10.3%) from Japan; and 5,538 (6.1%) from Britain.

The 116 member countries as of August 2002 were:

Albania	(AL)	Denmark	(DK)
Algeria	(DZ)	Dominica	(DO)
Antigua and Barbuda	(AG)	Ecuador	(EC)
Armenia	(AM)	Equatorial Guinea	(GQ)
Australia	(AU)	Estonia	(EE)
Austria	(AT)	Finland	(FI)
Azerbaijan	(AZ)	France	(FR)
Barbados	(BB)	Gabon	(GA)
Belarus	(BY)	Gambia	(GM)
Belgium	(BE)	Georgia	(GE)
Belize	(BZ)	Germany	(DE)
Benin	(BJ)	Ghana	(GH)
Bosnia and Herzegovina	(BA)	Greece	(GR)
Brazil	(BR)	Grenada	(GD)
Bulgaria	(BG)	Guinea	(GN)
Burkina Faso	(BF)	Guinea-Bissau	(GW)
Cameroon	(CM)	Hungary	(HU)
Canada	(CA)	Iceland	(IS)
Central African Republic	(CF)	India	(IN)
Chad	(TD)	Indonesia	(ID)
China	(CN)	Ireland	(IE)
Colombia	(CO)	Israel	(IL)
Congo	(CG)	Italy	(IT)
Costa Rica	(CR)	Japan	(JP)
Côte d'Ivoire	(CI)	Kazakhstan	(KZ)
Croatia	(HR)	Kenya	(KE)
Cuba	(CU)	Korea, Democratic People's	
Cyprus	(CY)	Republic of	(KP)
Czech Republic	(CZ)	Korea, Republic of	(KR)

Kyrgyzstan	(KG)	Saint Vincent	(VC)
Latvia	(LV)	Senegal	(SN)
Lesotho	(LS)	Sierra Leone	(SL)
Liberia	(LR)	Singapore	(SG)
Liechtenstein	(LI)	Slovakia	(SK)
Lithuania	(LT)	Slovenia	(SI)
Luxembourg	(LU)	South Africa	(ZA)
Macedonia, former Yugoslav		Spain	(ES)
Republic of	(MC)	Sri Lanka	(LK)
Madagascar	(MG)	Sudan	(SD)
Malawi	(MW)	Swaziland	(SZ)
Mali	(ML)	Sweden	(SE)
Mauritania	(MR)	Switzerland	(CH)
Mexico	(MX)	Tajikistan	(TJ)
Moldova	(MD)	Togo	(TG)
Monaco	(MC)	Trinidad and Tobago	(TT)
Mongolia	(MN)	Tunisia	(TN)
Morocco	(MA)	Turkey	(TR)
Mozambique	(MZ)	Turkmenistan	(TM)
Netherlands	(NL)	Uganda	(UG)
New Zealand	(NZ)	Ukraine	(UA)
Niger	(NE)	United Arab Emirates	(AE)
Norway	(NO)	United Kingdom	(GB)
Oman	(OM)	United Republic of Tanzania	(TZ)
Philippines	(PH)	United States of America	(US)
Poland	(PL)	Uzbekistan	(UZ)
Portugal	(PT)	Viet Nam	(VN)
Romania	(RO)	Yugoslavia	(YU)
Russian Federation	(RU)	Zambia	(ZM)
Saint Lucia	(LC)	Zimbabwe	(ZW)

Numeration and document codes

Patent applications are given a number such as PCT/US00/41724 when they are filed at a receiving office on behalf of the Patent Cooperation Treaty. Each receiving office allocates a number within an annual sequence. In the front page illustrated in Figure 2.2, INID code (21), US indicates that it was filed via the United States Patent and Trademark Office, 00 that it was filed in 2000, and 41724 is the consecutive number allocated by that local office. Nothing is published under these numbers. The code IB (rather than a country code) signifies a filing made directly to the International Bureau, that is, WIPO itself (probably because the local patent office does not act as a receiving office).

This application was published as WO 01/32386 A2. WO is the code for the World Intellectual Property Organization, and 01 indicates that it was published in 2001. 32386 is the number in a fresh sequence beginning at 1 each year. From 1 July 2002, however, there will be six digits following the year. From 1 January 2004 "the year" will be given four digitst, hence 2004/000001 onwards.

The document code A1 signifies that it was published with a search report at the end. A2 signifies that it was published without a search report. A3 signifies a separately published search report. There are less used codes as well: B1 is for amended claims, C1 a modified front page, C2 a completely corrected specification. These were used from 1999 with previous such publications lacking any codes.

The code W may be found against a PCT published number and a country code. This is usage by Inpadoc which means that that country has been designated in the PCT specification.

Patenting procedure

The patenting procedure is similar to that at the British and European Patent Offices in that the A specification is published 18 months after the priority date (see Figure 2.1). Unlike the British or European Patent Office procedures, however, there is no grant of a patent or republication of the specification. Applications are made by citizens or residents of member states. Filing is normally made via the local patent office which acts as a "receiving office".

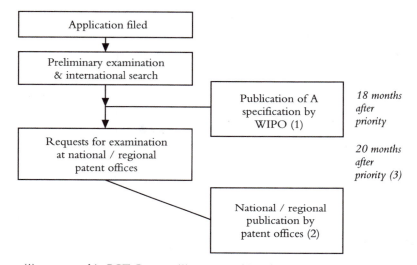

(1) = reported in PCT Gazette; (2) = reported in other gazettes
(3) = minimum 20 months (see text)

Figure 2.1. Procedure for applying under the Patent Cooperation Treaty

A search is carried out of one of the ten international searching authorities. These are Australia, Austria, China, the European Patent Office (EPO), Japan, Korea, Russia, Spain, Sweden and the USA. In 2000 60.9% of the searches were carried out by the EPO and 19.1% by the USA.

Applications for patents are published every week as PCT A specifications in one of the permitted languages. These languages, and the percentage published in that language in 2000, are English (70.2%), German (15.0%), Japanese (8.8%), French (4.6%), Russian (0.6%), Spanish (0.5%) and Chinese (0.3%). The publication is generally with a search report and occurs 18 months after the priority date. An English abstract is always provided even if the specification is in a foreign language and will always be on the front page (a foreign language abstract may go over to the second page).

After publication and assessment of the search report the applicant may abandon the application or proceed to obtain, as appropriate, a European or other regional patent and/or selected national patents in the states which were designated. This is referred to as entering the national or regional phase. Code (81) on the front page indicates the countries and code (84) the regional systems where protection is sought.

Although there is a procedure for obtaining an international preliminary examination under the Patent Co-operation Treaty (not shown in Figure 2.1) it is ultimately always necessary to apply separately to the national or regional patent offices for the grant of a patent. The advantages of using the PCT route to get international protection are the extra time it allows applicants to lodge their application in patent offices abroad; more time to assess the market and novelty of the invention; and therefore delaying (and perhaps preventing if not proceeding further) the considerable costs of translating the specification into languages acceptable to each jurisdiction. Generally the time limit under the PCT is 20 months (more if an international preliminary examination is requested) from the priority date compared with 12 months for filing abroad without using the PCT. From January 2002 the European Patent Office will allow 31 months from the priority date where a European Patent is requested.

Specifications

As with the European patent specification, the front page of the PCT specification contains bibliographic information, a list of designated states, an abstract and a significant drawing. A front page of a PCT application from the Coca-Cola Company, WO 01/32386 A2, is shown in Figure 2.2. Before 30 November 2000 the published specifications only had code (81) for designated states instead of dividing them as shown between code (81) for national designations and (84) for regional designations.

There will always be an English abstract on the front page. If the specification is not in a Roman script then the front page names, designated states and filing information are given in Roman script as well as in that language.

A search report similar to that given by the European Patent Office is given at the end of the A1 specifications or in a separately published A3 document. Some International Search Authorities add pages listing the patent families for the patents cited to assist those who cannot read the language of the cited patent.

There are no requirements for the applicant to supply a translation of the specification provided that it is published in one of the agreed languages. It is possible to file in another language provided that an appropriate translation is later provided. If the application proceeds to the national or regional phase then translations may be required and later published by the national or regional patent offices.

As well as publishing specifications on paper, they are put on the Web and on DVD-ROM. There are two files on the European Patent Office's **Esp@cenet** website, **http://gb.espacenet.com**, that can be used. The file labelled "The World Intellectual Property Org. (PCT)" contains details of patent applications issued in the two most recent years and the file labelled "Worldwide" contains all published PCT patent applications.

(12) INTERNATIONAL APPLICATION PUBLISHED UNDER THE PATENT COOPERATION TREATY (PCT)

(19) World Intellectual Property Organization
International Bureau

(43) International Publication Date
10 May 2001 (10.05.2001)

PCT

(10) International Publication Number
WO 01/32386 A2

(51) International Patent Classification[7]: B29C

(21) International Application Number: PCT/US00/41724

(22) International Filing Date:
1 November 2000 (01.11.2000)

(25) Filing Language: English

(26) Publication Language: English

(30) Priority Data:
09/432,339   2 November 1999 (02.11.1999)   US

(71) Applicant: THE COCA-COLA COMPANY [US/US];
One Coca-Cola Plaza, NW, Atlanta, GA 31313 (US).

(72) Inventor: LADINA, Joseph, M.; 2140 Cannon Way, Marietta, GA 30064 (US).

(74) Agents: BIRCH, Anthony, L.; Finnegan, Henderson, Farabow, Garrett & Dunner, L.L.P., 1300 I Street, NW , Washington, DC 20005-3315 et al. (US).

(81) Designated States *(national)*: AE, AG, AL, AM, AT, AU, AZ, BA, BB, BG, BR, BY, BZ, CA, CH, CN, CR, CU, CZ, DE, DK, DM, DZ, EE, ES, FI, GB, GD, GE, GH, GM, HR, HU, ID, IL, IN, IS, JP, KE, KG, KP, KR, KZ, LC, LK, LR, LS, LT, LU, LV, MA, MD, MG, MK, MN, MW, MX, MZ, NO, NZ, PL, PT, RO, RU, SD, SE, SG, SI, SK, SL, TJ, TM, TR, TT, TZ, UA, UG, UZ, VN, YU, ZA, ZW.

(84) Designated States *(regional)*: ARIPO patent (GH, GM, KE, LS, MW, MZ, SD, SL, SZ, TZ, UG, ZW), Eurasian patent (AM, AZ, BY, KG, KZ, MD, RU, TJ, TM), European patent (AT, BE, CH, CY, DE, DK, ES, FI, FR, GB, GR, IE, IT, LU, MC, NL, PT, SE, TR), OAPI patent (BF, BJ, CF, CG, CI, CM, GA, GN, GW, ML, MR, NE, SN, TD, TG).

[Continued on next page]

(54) Title: IMPROVED APPARATUS AND METHOD FOR CONCEALING A PROMOTIONAL COMPARTMENT

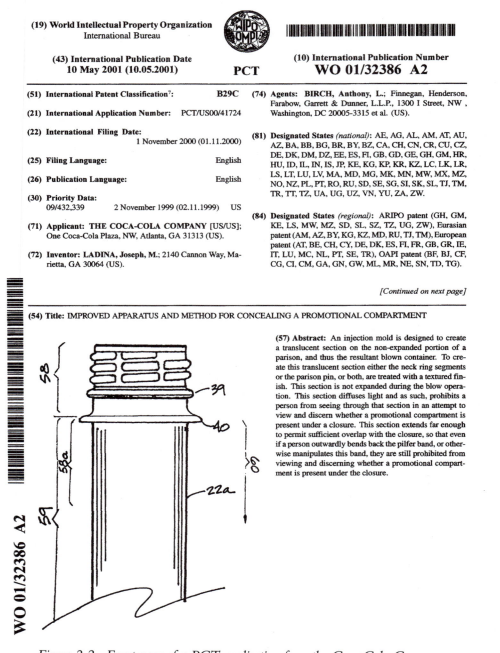

(57) Abstract: An injection mold is designed to create a translucent section on the non-expanded portion of a parison, and thus the resultant blown container. To create this translucent section either the neck ring segments or the parison pin, or both, are treated with a textured finish. This section is not expanded during the blow operation. This section diffuses light and as such, prohibits a person from seeing through that section in an attempt to view and discern whether a promotional compartment is present under a closure. This section extends far enough to permit sufficient overlap with the closure, so that even if a person outwardly bends back the pilfer band, or otherwise manipulates this band, they are still prohibited from viewing and discerning whether a promotional compartment is present under the closure.

WO 01/32386 A2

Figure 2.2. Front page of a PCT application from the Coca-Cola Company

Alternatively, the PCT database within the World Intellectual Property Organization "Intellectual Property Digital Library" (**http://ipdl.wipo.int/en**) can be searched and is more flexible than the **Esp@cenet** service but is only for publications from January 1997.

The European Patent Office produce a CD-ROM (or DVD-ROM) database which covers PCT applications. ACCESS contains front page data (except for drawings) and can be used as a search tool for all EP and Patent Co-operation Treaty applications.

There are a number of value-added databases which provide searchable information on PCT applications and others which incorporate them including the Derwent and Inpadoc services mentioned on pages 107 and 108.

Abstracts

The published *PCT Gazette* formerly published English abstracts and drawings in numerical order for all PCT publications but this coverage ceased with April 1998. Derwent Information's *World patent abstracts* has its own abstracts of the PCT applications and is arranged by Derwent classes.

The PCT Electronic Gazette Database at **http://ipdl.wipo.int/en** provides from January 1997 only front page data and drawings and can be searched by all elements. It is updated on day of publication. The **Esp@cenet** database at **http://gb.espacenet.com** contains all PCT abstracts but the "worldwide" option should be chosen as the coverage is longer than the "PCT" option and it allows the abstracts and not just the titles to be searched.

The ACCESS CD-ROM produced by the European Patent Office allows searching of PCT abstracts.

The Gazette

The weekly *PCT Gazette* is published in English and contains details of PCT specifications which are published on the same day as the Gazette. Official notices that were formerly published in the *PCT Gazette* have since March 1994 been published monthly as the *PCT Newsletter* (also available online from 1997 at **http://www.wipo.org/pct/en/newslett**).

The PCT applications are not granted without being applied for at a national or regional patent office and there is no information made available by WIPO subsequent to the publication of the application. It can be difficult to determine whether a PCT application has entered (or not entered) the national or regional phases in particular countries since there is no single database which records this. The Inpadoc legal status database (see page 108) records this information for some countries but for others it may be necessary to view the registers of the individual offices.

The British Library and the PCT applications

The British Library maintains a complete set of PCT documents in numerical order on paper and in digital form. Separately laid out each week is a set of the current week's published patent applications on paper. They are set out in numerical order which, since it is a classified subject order, allows subject searching. The Library also holds information on the Patent Cooperation Treaty processes, procedures and output.

Internet databases

The official database is the *PCT Electronic Gazette* at **http://ipdl.wipo.int/en**. This provides bibliographic data, an abstract and drawing from January 1997 onwards on the day of publication (Thursday) plus images of the complete specification after a delay of about two weeks.

The **Esp@cenet** database at **http://gb.espacenet.com** provides on its "worldwide" option images of all PCT specifications. They can be searched by the usual bibliographic data.

The free Delphion site at **http://www.delphion.com/simple** unlike the two listed above both acknowledged the existence of, and provided a copy of, the A3 corresponding to WO 9920000 A2.

Because of the importance of the PCT, and its pervasiveness elsewhere with the national and regional phase, PCT data is to be found in many other databases, including priced sites.

Contact information

World Intellectual Property Organization
34, chemin des Colombettes
1211 Geneva 20
Switzerland

Tel: +41 (0) 22 338 9111
Fax: +41 (0) 22 733 5428

Web address [for the PCT]: **http://www.wipo.org/pct/en/index.html**

Further reading

PCT Applicants' Guide. World Intellectual Property Organization [besides printed version, on web at **http://www.wipo.int/pct/guide/en**].

Patent Co-operation Treaty and regulations. Located at **http://www.wipo.org/treaties/registration/index.html**.

The first twenty-five years of the Patent Cooperation Treaty (PCT), 1970-1995, World Intellectual Property Organization. Geneva: WIPO, 1995.

Patent Cooperation Treaty Handbook. C. Jones and the Chartered Institute of Patent Agents. London: FT Law and Tax, 1997-.

3. THE EUROPEAN PATENT CONVENTION

The European Patent Convention (EPC), under which applications for patents have been made since 1978, enables patents to be obtained in numerous designated European countries following a single application which may be submitted in one of the three working languages, English, French or German. It is administered by the European Patent Office (EPO) in Munich, Germany.

In the year 2000 there were 96,023 published application numbers assigned by the EPO. Not all of these were actual publications, as 62% of all filings were "Euro–PCTs" which were first filed through the Patent Cooperation Treaty and which later entered the regional European phase as a result of the EPC being designated in the publication. They were assigned a "ghost" number if the original were in one of the EPC working languages. They were published in translation if the PCT publication were not in one of the EPC working languages. The remainder were filed directly at the EPO. About half the filings were from member states and the rest were mainly American or Japanese. In 1999 27,523 patents were granted.

In 1990 there had been 62,778 filings of which only 16% were Euro-PCTs. 24,757 patents were granted.

The member countries of the Convention are, as of July 2002:

Austria	(AT)
Belgium	(BE)
Bulgaria	(BG)
Cyprus	(CY)
Czech Republic	(CZ)
Denmark	(DK)
Estonia	(EE)
Finland	(FI)
France	(FR)
Germany	(DE)
Greece	(GR)
Ireland	(IE)
Italy	(IT)
Liechtenstein	(LI)
Luxembourg	(LU)
Monaco	(MC)
Netherlands	(NL)
Portugal	(PT)
Slovakia	(SK)
Spain	(ES)
Sweden	(SE)
Switzerland	(CH)
Turkey	(TR)
United Kingdom	(GB)

In addition there are a number of other countries, called extension states, in which European Patents can have effect. As of July 2002 these were:

Albania	(AL)
Latvia	(LV)
Lithuania	(LT)
Macedonia, former Yugoslav Republic of	(MK)
Romania	(RO)
Slovenia	(SI)

An applicant for a patent can designate any of the member states and any of the extension states for patent protection. The country codes are shown on the specifications as "Designated Contracting States" in INID code (84), and from 22 January 1997 any such designations of extension states are printed in the specifications as a separate list of "Designated Extension States" in INID code (84).

Numeration and document codes

Applications are given a number such as 98929864.1 when they are filed at the EPO. The first two digits are the last two digits of the year of filing. The following two indicate the office where it was initially filed (this may be a suboffice or a national office) with the following digits being an annual sequence for that office. The digit after the decimal point is a check digit. The numbering of published applications is continuous, beginning at EP 0 000 001. This number is retained if the patent is granted. The first number assigned to a published patent application in 2001 was EP 1 063 877 (which was not actually published as it was filed through the PCT).

Each published document bears a code. The main codes are for the applications. A1 means published with a search report, A2 means published without a search report, and A3 means a separately published search report. B1 signifies a granted patent. All the codes used are given below.

Al	First publication of the specification with search report
A2	First publication of the specification without search report
A3	Later publication of search report with revised front page of specification
A4	Publication of Supplementary Search Report [not actually published except on Internet]
A8	Republication of corrected title page of first publication
A9	Republication of complete first publication
Bl	Second publication of the specification, the granted patent
B2	Amended granted patent resulting from an opposition
B8	Republication of corrected title page of granted patent
B9	Republication of complete granted patent

The code R may be found against a European number and a country code. This is usage by Inpadoc which means that that country has been designated in the European specification.

Patenting procedure

The patenting procedure is similar to that in the UK in that the A specification is published 18 months after the priority date. Examination is on request within six months of publication of the search report and, if accepted, the specification is published a second time on grant (B specification). The procedure is illustrated in Figure 3.1.

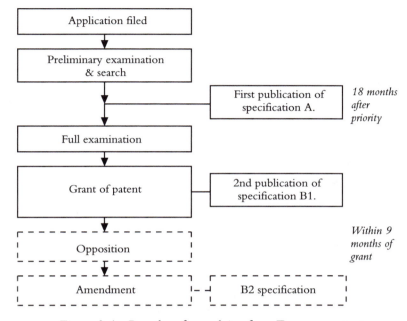

Figure 3.1. Procedure for applying for a European patent

The first applications were filed on 1 June 1978, the first specifications were published in December 1978 and the first patents granted in April 1980. About 70% are published in English.

A specifications, in English, French or German, are published weekly in numerical order on Wednesdays. If an application for a European Patent is made by first applying under the Patent Cooperation Treaty (PCT) (see Chapter 2) and the PCT specification is in English, French or German, it will not be republished by the European Patent Office although it will be given a number in the continuous sequence of published European Patent applications. To find the specification for one of these "Euro-PCT" applications not published as a European application the sequence of PCT documents must be consulted. Those PCT applications made in any other language will be published in translation in one of the three official languages by the EPO. The patent applicant normally has eight months after publication of the Patent Co-operation Treaty application to apply for a European Patent so the assignment of a number to a PCT application entering the European phase is typically delayed by 8-12 months. The time limit was extended from the beginning of 2002 and further details are given in Chapter 2.

The granted patents (B specification) are also published weekly in the original language but the claims are in all three languages: English, French and German. The granted patent should contain no technical disclosure which was not in the corresponding A specification but is important in that it defines the scope of the protection given by the patent.

Opposition to granted patents can be initiated within nine months of grant. The opposition is then considered by the EPO. Opposition taking place after the nine month period must be pursued separately through the national courts in the designated countries.

Renewal fees are paid to the individual patent offices in the designated states, since the patents are treated after grant as separate national patents. The patent can be allowed to lapse in some countries while it continues to be protected in others. The maximum term of protection is 20 years from the filing date at the European Patent Office with the possibility of an extension (known as a Supplementary Protection Certificate or SPC) in individual countries for patents on pharmaceutical and plant protection products.

Specifications

Immediately following the publication number on the front of a European Patent document is the "kind of document" code comprising one letter and one digit. The main codes are A1, published with a search report, A2, published without a search report and A3, separately published search report. B1 is the normal code for a grant.

The front page of the first published A specification contains bibliographic information, including the designated states, an abstract and a significant drawing where appropriate. The search report may be published with the specification or separately later. A Supplementary Search report, an A4, is sometimes "published" to enhance the Euro-PCT report. They are available on the web at the **Esp@cenet** database at **http://gb.espacenet.com** and are given as part of the patent family for each invention. Corrected application documents may be republished with A8 or A9 codes.

The front page of a European patent application, EP 0 636 338 A2, is given in Figure 3.2. It is an application for a patent on a vacuum cleaner component invented by James Dyson. The features of the front page are similar to those on a British patent application but the designated states listing the countries in which patent protection is sought are given.

Those Euro-PCTs which are published in translation bear near the top, below "European patent application", the words "Published in accordance with Art. 158 (3) EPC". Code (87) gives the PCT publication number.

From January 1999 both published applications and grants have had the paragraphs in the descriptions numbered in the format [0001], [0002], etc.

For a few years while Greece and Spain were members of the EPC but not of the PCT any filings made through the PCT would designate the other states within an EP while a second application was made direct to the EPO for a European patent for just those two states. If such a publication is found it almost certainly means that a second EP number, corresponding to the original PCT, will be found.

The amended front page of the original A2 document is reprinted along with the search report as an A3 publication when the search has been carried out. The search report from the vacuum cleaner patent application (without its title page) is shown in Figure 3.4. The search report is always at the end of the specification in an A1 specification.

(19) **Europäisches Patentamt**

European Patent Office

Office européen des brevets

(11) Publication number: **0 636 338 A2**

(12) **EUROPEAN PATENT APPLICATION**

(21) Application number: 94117238.9

(22) Date of filing: 03.12.91

(51) Int. Cl.6: **A47L 9/16**

This application was filed on 02 - 11 - 1994 as a divisional application to the application mentioned under INID code 60.

(30) Priority: 03.12.90 US 621375

(43) Date of publication of application:
01.02.95 Bulletin 95/05

(60) Publication number of the earlier application in accordance with Art.76 EPC: **0 489 565**

(84) Designated Contracting States:
AT BE CH DE DK ES FR GB GR IT LI LU NL SE

(71) Applicant: **NOTETRY LIMITED**
Sycamore House
Bathford
Bath BA1 7RS (GB)

(72) Inventor: **Dyson, James**
Sycamore House,
Bathford
Bath,
Avon BA1 7RS (GB)

(74) Representative: **Smith, Gillian Ruth**
MARKS & CLERK,
57-60 Lincoln's Inn Fields
London WC2A 3LS (GB)

(54) **Shroud and cyclonic cleaning apparatus incorporating same.**

(57) A shroud for use in a dual inner and outer cyclonic vacuum cleaner (10) is described. The shroud has a cylindrical section (50c, 132) adjacent an inner surface 15b, 111b) of a cyclonic container (15,111) and preferably comprises a combined shroud disc unit (50). The combined shroud and disc unit fits on the outside surface (20c) of the inner cyclone (20) and aids in removal of first and fibrous matter from the airflow in the outer cyclone (15). Improved airflow between the outer cyclone (15) and inner cyclone (20) is achieved because of the shroud and disc unit (50).

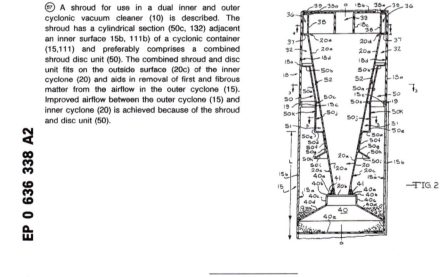

EP 0 636 338 A2

Figure 3.2. Application for a patent on a vacuum cleaner component

Search reports by the European Patent Office, the Patent Cooperation Treaty, Britain and France now have a similar (but not identical) appearance. At the bottom of the page appear notes interpreting the codes used in the actual report. Broadly speaking, the significance of the main codes are:

A = background, will not invalidate the invention
X = not novel, likely to invalidate at least part of the invention
Y = obvious, likely to invalidate at least part of the invention

Hence in the Dyson search report the first column, category, is A, background as regards GB 469539 which applies to Claim 1 of the application in question. If a particular claim is known to be of interest it can be looked up in the search report to see if it turns up. With no X or Y citations against this application it appeared to be new, but care should always be taken in interpreting a search report. Without the help of a patent agent or the relevant patent office examiner (whose name is usually given) this is difficult and can be dangerous if decisions are taken as a result of faulty interpretation.

The front page of granted patent EP 0 636 338 B1 is given in Figure 3.3. There is a summary of the patent application's search report at INID code (56). No abstract or drawing is given on the front page. The title at code (54) is given in all three official languages, as are the claims.

If the B1 is of a Euro-PCT then the PCT publication number is given at code (87).

The European Patent Office, as well as publishing specifications on paper, publishes them on the web and on CD-ROM. There are two files on the European Patent Office's **Esp@cenet** website at **http://gb.espacenet.com** that can be used. The file labelled "The European Patent Office" contains details of patent applications issued in the two most recent years and the file labelled "Worldwide" includes all European patent applications.

The European Patent Office produces three main CD-ROM (or DVD-ROM) databases which cover European patents or patent applications. ACCESS EP-A contains front page data of published applications (except for drawings, and can be used as a search tool) and ACCESS EP-B contains claims of granted patents plus other bibliographic data. BULLETIN contains brief data without abstracts or drawings but contains status information on published applications and grants.

Abstracts

Each published application has an abstract on the front page, in the same language as the specification. There are a number of sources for an English language abstract. These can include (if the original were published through the Patent Cooperation Treaty) the original published application in that system, which will always have an English abstract on the front page. Other sources involve a delay in preparing the abstract. The **Esp@cenet** database at **http://gb.espacenet.com/** has abstracts. There is also Derwent Information's careful abstracts which are printed in their European Abstracts, Unexamined patent number order series. These are the same as those on their priced online database.

The gazette and register

The *European Patent Bulletin* has been issued from December 1979 on the same day as the patent specifications. It lists separately all the published applications and granted patents that have been issued. There are also lists by publication number, application number, name of applicant, designated states and PCT number, where applicable. The *Bulletin* provides a weekly concordance between the application number and publication number. Announcements of any oppositions filed against European patents and their outcome are also noted in the *Bulletin*.

(19) Europäisches Patentamt
European Patent Office
Office européen des brevets

(11) **EP 0 636 338 B1**

(12) **EUROPEAN PATENT SPECIFICATION**

(45) Date of publication and mention of the grant of the patent:
11.06.1997 Bulletin 1997/24

(51) Int. Cl.[6]: **A47L 9/16**

(21) Application number: **94117238.9**

(22) Date of filing: **03.12.1991**

(54) **Shroud and cyclonic cleaning apparatus incorporating same**
Umhüllung und damit versehene Zyklonstaubsauger
Enveloppe et aspirateur cyclone muni de celle-ci

(84) Designated Contracting States:
AT BE CH DE DK ES FR GB GR IT LI LU NL SE

(30) Priority: **03.12.1990 US 621375**

(43) Date of publication of application:
01.02.1995 Bulletin 1995/05

(62) Document number(s) of the earlier application(s) in accordance with Art. 76 EPC:
91311229.8 / 0 489 565

(73) Proprietor: **NOTETRY LIMITED**
Little Somerford, Wiltshire SN15 5JN (GB)

(72) Inventor: **Dyson, James**
Bath, Avon BA1 7RS (GB)

(74) Representative: **Smith, Gillian Ruth**
MARKS & CLERK,
57-60 Lincoln's Inn Fields
London WC2A 3LS (GB)

(56) References cited:

GB-A- 469 539	US-A- 4 571 772
US-A- 4 573 236	US-A- 4 593 429
US-A- 4 643 748	US-A- 4 826 515
US-A- 4 853 008	US-A- 4 853 011

EP 0 636 338 B1

Note: Within nine months from the publication of the mention of the grant of the European patent, any person may give notice to the European Patent Office of opposition to the European patent granted. Notice of opposition shall be filed in a written reasoned statement. It shall not be deemed to have been filed until the opposition fee has been paid. (Art. 99(1) European Patent Convention).

Printed by Rank Xerox (UK) Business Services
2.14.7/3.4

Figure 3.3. Front page of a European grant

European Patent Office	EUROPEAN SEARCH REPORT	Application Number EP 94 11 7238

DOCUMENTS CONSIDERED TO BE RELEVANT

Category	Citation of document with indication, where appropriate, of relevant passages	Relevant to claim	CLASSIFICATION OF THE APPLICATION (Int.Cl.5)
A	GB-A-469 539 (BRITISH THOMSON-HOUSTON CY LTD) * the whole document * ---	1	A47L9/16
D,A	US-A-4 853 008 (J. DYSON) * the whole document * ---	1,14	
D,A	US-A-4 593 429 (J. DYSON) * the whole document * ---	1,14	
D,A	US-A-4 643 748 (J. DYSON) * the whole document * ---	1,14	
D,A	US-A-4 826 515 (J. DYSON) * the whole document * ---	1,14	
D,A	US-A-4 853 011 (J. DYSON) * the whole document * ---	1,14	
D,A	US-A-4 571 772 (J. DYSON) * the whole document * ---	14	TECHNICAL FIELDS SEARCHED (Int.Cl.5)
D,A	US-A-4 573 236 (J. DYSON) * the whole document * -----	14	A47L

The present search report has been drawn up for all claims

Place of search	Date of completion of the search	Examiner
THE HAGUE	27 March 1995	Vanmol, M

CATEGORY OF CITED DOCUMENTS

X : particularly relevant if taken alone
Y : particularly relevant if combined with another document of the same category
A : technological background
O : non-written disclosure
P : intermediate document

T : theory or principle underlying the invention
E : earlier patent document, but published on, or after the filing date
D : document cited in the application
L : document cited for other reasons

& : member of the same patent family, corresponding document

EPO FORM 1503 03.82 (P04C01)

Figure 3.4. European search report

All of this information is cumulated in the official (and free) register which is known as Epoline® on the web at **http://www.epoline.org**. Below is given the information that is available on Epoline® for the James Dyson patent shown earlier.

Online European Patent Register - Results

Status of the database as of 12-07-2001 (dd-mm-yyyy)

Choose your View:

     All data mentioned in Rule 92 and EPIDOS

Publication numbers, publication type and publication dates

	EP0636338 A2 01-02-1995 [1995/05]
	EP0636338 A3 17-05-1995 [1995/20]
	EP0636338 B1 11-06-1997 [1997/24]
Date of grant	11-06-1997 [1997/24]

Application numbers and filing date

	EP19940117238 (94117238.9)
Date of filing	03-12-1991 [1995/05]

Date of publication of search report	17-05-1995 [1995/20]
Priority number, priority date	US19900621375 03-12-1990 [1995/05]
Classification (IPC)	A47L9/16 [1995/05]
Designated states	AT , BE , CH , DE , DK , ES , FR , GB , GR , IT , LI , LU , NL , SE [1995/05]
English title	Shroud and cyclonic cleaning apparatus incorporating same [1995/05]
French title	Enveloppe et aspirateur cyclone muni de celle-ci [1995/05]
German title	Umhüllung und damit versehene Zyklonstaubsauger [1995/05]
Designated states, applicant name, address	FOR ALL DESIGNATED STATES NOTETRY LIMITED Kingsmead Mill Little Somerford, Wiltshire SN15 5JN/GB [1997/09]
Inventor name, address	01/Dyson, James/Kingsmead Mill/Little Somerford, Wiltshire SN15 5JN / GB [1997/42]
Representative name, address	Smith, Gillian Ruth MARKS & CLERK, 57-60 Lincoln's Inn Fields London WC2A 3LS/GB [1995/05]
Filing language	EN
Procedure language	EN
Publication language	
B1	EN [1997/24]
A2	EN [1995/05]

Location of file and fax number for file inspection requests

    Application is treated in (/fax-nr)   MUNICH/(+49-89) 23994465

Examination procedure

request for examination   18-11-1994 [1995/05]
Examination report(s)   A.96(2), R.51(2)
date dispatch/time-limit/reply   28-05-1996/M04/30-09-1996
communication R.51(4)   05-11-1996
dispatched
– approval (yes or no)   yes
communication R.51(6)   05-12-1996
dispatched
payment of fee for grant/ 18-02-1997/18-02-1997
fee for printing

Earlier Application

Parent application/   EP19910311229/EP0489565 [1995/05]
publication number(s)

Opposition procedure

no opposition filed,   12-03-1998 [1998/23]
time-limit expired on

Renewal fees

Renewal fee A.86   03/18-11-1994
(patent year / paid)   04/18-11-1994
                          05/08-12-1995
                          06/11-12-1996

Lapsed, data supplied by contracting states

AT/11-06-1997
BE/11-06-1997
CH/11-06-1997
DK/11-06-1997
GR/11-06-1997
LI/11-06-1997
LU/31-12-1997 [2000/05]

Documents cited in the European Search

GB469539 A [A];
US4853008 A [AD];
US4593429 A [AD];
US4643748 A [AD];
US4826515 A [AD];
US4853011 A [AD];
US4571772 A [AD];
US4573236 A [AD]

[End of Data]

[results page from EPOLINE]

An alternative source for cumulated information from the Bulletin is the BULLETIN CD-ROM product.

Information on the status of European Patents designating the United Kingdom after grant is given in the British *Patents and Designs Journal* and in the UK patent register on the web (see Chapter 4).

Translations

Designated states require applicants to submit translations of the claims in European Patent applications into the official language of the country before protection becomes fully effective in that state and to submit translations of the entire granted European patent to prevent the patent being declared void. The Patents (Amendment) Rules 1987 introduced this provision in the United Kingdom for applications published and patents granted after 1 September 1987. These translations are made available by the British Patent Office and are also held at the British Library. The date of filing translations is given in the UK patent register on the web. The requirement for translations may be limited in future if the London Protocol to the European Patent Convention comes into force (see **http://www.ige.ch/E/jurinfo/pdf/epc65_e.pdf** which would revise Article 65).

Case law

Oppositions can be lodged against decisions made by the European Patent Office and will be examined by Appeal Boards. The decisions are published (generally in the language of the hearing) on the ESPACE-LEGAL CD-ROM. The text of every decision despatched from June 1993 is available on the European Patent Office website at **http://www.european-patent-office.org/dg3/search_dg3.htm**. Certain of the decisions are published in English, French and German in the *Official Journal* of the European Patent Office, which is itself on the European Patent Office website at **http://www.european-patent-office.org/epo/pubs/oj_index_e.htm**. The *Official Journal* of the European Patent Office also contains official notices from the European Patent Office.

Status data is on the official Epoline® database at **http://www.epoline.org**. This does not go beyond the opposition period. It is planned that it will link to copies of the actual file wrappers (correspondence etc.) of published European applications.

Other official databases are listed under "European" within the British Library's list of links at **http://www.bl.uk/services/information/patents/othlink2.html#singe**.

The British Library and the European Patent Convention patents

The British Library maintains a complete set of EP A documents in numerical order and for those Euro-PCT applications which are not reprinted by the EPO, it substitutes copies of the front pages of the corresponding PCT applications. Separately laid out each week is a set of the current week's published patent applications. They are set out in numerical order which, since it is in classified subject order, allows subject searching. The last three weeks' B specifications are kept in separate boxes at the British Library to facilitate searching. The Library also provides access to digitised copies of the specifications, databases and European Patent Office procedures and output.

As explained in the section "Translations" the British Library has a set of translations of European grants which designate Britain and which were in German or French.

Internet databases

Esp@cenet at **http://gb.espacenet.com** is the official database and can be used for simple searches of European Patents. Most of the front page (bibliographic) data can be searched and the complete specification can be viewed.

There are a number of value-added databases which provide searchable text of European Patents and others which incorporate European Patents including the Derwent and Inpadoc services mentioned elsewhere (see pages 107–8). The Inpadoc service, both in the form of CD-ROM and online services, give status information on European Patents up to and after grant. The priced Delphion service at **http://www.delphion.com/simple** provides status data for specific European patents up to the opposition.

Status data is on the official Epoline® database at **http://www.epoline.org**. This does not go beyond the opposition period. It is planned that it will link to copies of the actual file wrappers (correspondence etc.) of published European applications.

Contact information

European Patent Office
Erhardtstrasse 27
D–80331 Munich
Germany

Tel: +49 (0) 89 2399 0
Fax: +49 (0) 89 2399 4465

Web address: **http://www.european-patent-office.org**

Further reading

How to get a European patent: the guide for applicants. European Patent Office. Located at **http://www.european-patent-office.org/ap_gd/index.htm**.

National law relating to the EPC. European Patent Office. Located at **http://www. european-patent-office.org/legal/national/index.htm**.

European Patent Convention. Located at **http://www.european-patent-office.org/ legal/epc/index.html**.

Guidelines for examination before the EPO. Located at **http://www.european-patent-office.org/legal/gui_lines/index.htm**.

Hearing 1997: on the future patent information policy of the European Patent Office. J. F. Sibley, *World Patent Information*, 1997, 19 (2), 87-92.

European patents: what is going on? C. Lees, *Patent World*, 1998, (103), 19-24.

Oppositions before the European Patent Office. G. Roberts, *Intellectual Property Quarterly*, 1999, (3), 304-330.

The European patent system: an introduction for patent searchers. N. Akers, *World Patent Information*, 1999, 21 (3), 135-163.

European Patent Office: the question of power. C. Lees, *Patent World*, 1999, (118), 23-26.

Diplomatic Conference for the Revision of the European Patent Convention, Munich 20-29 November 2000. R. Nack and B. Phelip, *IIC*, 2001, 32 (2), 200-208.

Status of revision of the European Patent Convention (EPC) and the draft EU Community patent. H. Goddar, *Patent World*, 2001, (131), 16-18.

4.   THE BRITISH PATENT SYSTEM

In the year 1999 there were 30,467 applications for patents filed at the British Patent Office. 12,043 patent specifications were published as patent applications and 7,995 were published as grants. Of these three totals, 69%, 44% and 36% respectively were of British origin. This chapter covers only British national patents, and the alternative way of protecting inventions in Britain, by using the European Patent Convention, is covered in Chapter 3.

Numeration and document codes

Between 1916 and 1 June 1978 British specifications were numbered by the Patent Office consecutively from 100,001 to about 1,600,000. These "old law" specifications were "sealed", or granted, after publication if fees were paid. A few inventions filed before 1978 are still being published under this old format and numeration. These are mostly militarily sensitive inventions.

Under both the old and the new law patent applications are given a number like 9103456 when they are filed at the Patent Office. The first two digits are the last two digits of the year of filing and the remaining five are a number from a sequence that begins from 1 each year. No specifications are numbered by these filing numbers. For the year 2000 the initial digits were 00 hence 0000001 was used for the first number allocated in that year.

Since 1 June 1978 applications have generally been published 18 months from the priority date (there can be exceptions) in a sequence beginning with 2,000,001 and with an A at the end. On grant they are republished, usually in modified form, with the identical publication number but with a B at the end. The first application to be published in 2001 was numbered GB 2351428 A (the Patent Office on its specifications prefers the format 2 351 428). If a B specification needs to be modified (probably after litigation) then the modified portion only is republished with the document code C.

AO is an informal code used by the Inpadoc database to indicate published information about the actual filing (as reported in the *Journal*).

Patenting procedure

The current British patenting procedure is illustrated in Figure 4.1. This procedure was laid down by the 1977 Patents Act. The actual filing of the patent application is now free.

British law requires British residents to file first at the British Patent Office even if no British patent is required. This is because the Ministry of Defence will intervene if the invention appears to be of a militarily sensitive nature. Some applications are as a result held in limbo, or are purchased compulsorily by the government. This initial filing need not include the claims, which can be filed at 12 months, but must be based on the specification as filed. Extra material would mean a refiling with a new priority date.

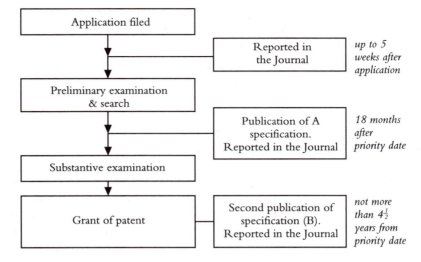

Journal = *Patents and Designs Journal*

Figure 4.1. Progress of a UK patent application under the Patents Act 1977

Otherwise, brief details are published in the official *Journal* (the *Patents and Designs Journal*) about five weeks after filing. These details consist of applicant's name, title, filing date and number, and any priority details. The title may be vague, but a clearer title may be required when it is published. Britain is the only major patenting authority that releases information so quickly. In most countries it is necessary to wait until the application (or sometimes a granted patent) is published.

A "preliminary examination and search" of the patent is also carried out. The preliminary examination is to see if the application has been set out correctly. If necessary the applicant will be told to reapply with a correct version within 12 months of the original application.

The applicant may also be told by the Patent Office to divide the application into two or more patent applications, or (less likely) to merge two or more patent applications into one.

The search consists of the examiner looking for patents or other published material which suggest that the invention in question is not new, or only an obvious improvement, at the time of the priority date (foreign priority date or else the first British filing date). A detailed search report together with copies of cited documents is sent to the applicant, who may wish to withdraw the application before publication because of an unfavourable report. The applicant may also withdraw the application for other (unstated) reasons. The Patent Office will not actually reject any applications at this stage because of the search report. If the application is not published then it and its associated file remains confidential and is destroyed five years after the date of filing.

British patent applications are published weekly on Wednesday (official holidays may disrupt this). The week's applications are arranged in British classified order to assist current awareness searchers. The application includes a list of citations from the search report. From 1 April 1992 the complete search report, similar to the European reports described on page 23, is published at the back of the application. The patent application is published about 18 months after the priority date, and hence perhaps only six months after the date of filing if it were originally applied for abroad. On the rare occasions when publication is delayed much beyond the 18 month period the invention is usually of a militarily sensitive nature. Again the *Journal* reports on the publication.

At this stage the patent is often called an unexamined, or A specification. It is not yet legally protected. It is from this date of publication of the specification that the file of correspondence between the Patent Office and the applicant, often called the "file wrapper", is available to interested parties.

The applicant then has six months in which to apply for a substantive examination, or it is deemed to have been withdrawn. Substantive examination involves the Patent Office examiner taking into account the citations in the search report plus the criteria needed for a patent to be valid, such as being useful, and deciding whether or not to grant a patent. Interested parties may also make objections to the application as a result of seeing the published application. The search report may suggest that part or all of the patent is not new, or is merely obvious, and the examiner may refuse the application, or insist on its modification. The claims in particular may need to be modified, or reduced in number.

If the patent is accepted, then it is published again, if necessary in modified form, as a B, or granted specification. Again it is reported in the *Journal*. The aim is to try to complete the procedure in four and a half years from the priority date. The only fees payable are one for the preliminary examination and search and another for the substantive examination.

Sometimes the granted patent is later attacked in court by others on the grounds that it is not new or is not a patentable concept. This can take place at any time after grant. If the action is partially successful, then the revised or deleted claims are given on an additional C document. A totally successful attack means that the patent will be revoked.

From 3 July 1995 an "accelerated processing of patent applications" procedure has been possible by which the preliminary and substantive examination stages can be performed together. This means a faster examination and grant is possible. The A document is published as normal but the B is often published only a few months later.

Protection for the patent is 20 years from the date of filing in the UK, subject to renewal fees being paid annually (which is from five years of filing in Britain). If the renewal fees are not paid then it lapses, while if it runs the full term then it is said to have expired. Supplementary Protection Certificates (SPCs) have been available for pharmaceutical patents from 1992 and for pesticides and fertilizers from 1997. These give a further term of protection to allow for the loss of time while authorities are checking for dangers to health. The patent must be "worked" within three years of grant or compulsory licensing to anyone interested will be forced on the applicant.

Specifications

Figure 4.2 shows the front page of British patent application GB 2 355 743 A. That is the correct citation: GB is the recognized country code for the United Kingdom, 2 355 743 is the number given to the published document, and A shows that it is the first, application stage of publication.

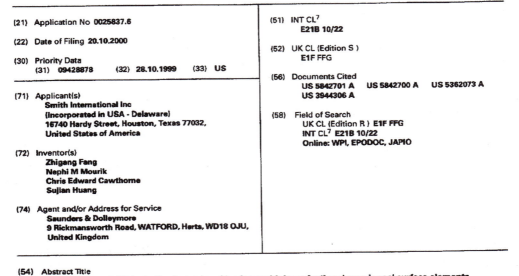

(12) **UK Patent Application** (19) **GB** (11) **2 355 743** (13) **A**

(43) Date of A Publication 02.05.2001

(21) Application No 0025837.6

(22) Date of Filing 20.10.2000

(30) Priority Data
(31) 09428878 (32) 28.10.1999 (33) US

(71) Applicant(s)
Smith International Inc
(Incorporated in USA - Delaware)
16740 Hardy Street, Houston, Texas 77032,
United States of America

(72) Inventor(s)
Zhigang Fang
Nephi M Mourik
Chris Edward Cawthorne
Sujian Huang

(74) Agent and/or Address for Service
Saunders & Dolleymore
9 Rickmansworth Road, WATFORD, Herts, WD18 OJU,
United Kingdom

(51) INT CL⁷
E21B 10/22

(52) UK CL (Edition S)
E1F FFG

(56) Documents Cited
US 5842701 A   US 5842700 A   US 5362073 A
US 3944306 A

(58) Field of Search
UK CL (Edition R) E1F FFG
INT CL⁷ E21B 10/22
Online: WPI, EPODOC, JAPIO

(54) Abstract Title
Rotary cone rock bit including journal seal having multiple projecting dynamic seal surface elements

(57) A rotary cone rock bit includes a bit body, a journal, a cutter cone rotatably mounted on the journal and an annular seal 33 forming a lubricant seal between the cone and journal. The seal has a static seal surface 56 and a dynamic seal surface 58 which includes two outwardly projecting surface elements 54, 55 separated by a recessed portion 68, one of the surface elements including a wear surface 72 formed of composite material. In a different form, at least one of the seal surface elements is formed of the same material as the seal body or another surface element and the seal ring has an aspect ratio greater than one. In another form, the surface elements are each formed of the same material which is different to that used to form the seal body. In yet another form, at least one of the surface elements is formed of a different material to that of the seal body and further includes a wear surface. In yet another form, the rotary dynamic surface of either the cutter cone or journal includes a raised portion that locates in the seal recessed portion.

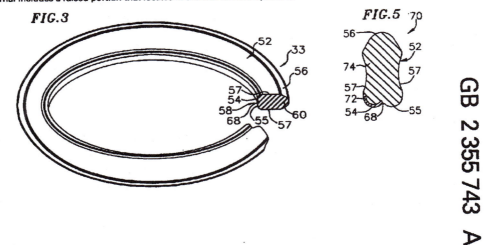

GB 2 355 743 A

Figure 4.2. *Front page of a British application*

The numbers in brackets are called INID codes. Besides helping to structure the bibliographic details, they are useful if the patent is in a foreign language, since e.g. code (72) would always mean the name of the inventor.

At the top right is the date of publication, 2 May 2001. On the left appears code (21), with the application number, 0025837. The number after the full stop, 6, is a check digit for computer purposes and is not normally required in searching. Code (22) gives the filing date in the format days, months, years.

The priority data takes up codes (31) to (33). From left to right they are the application number, the priority filing date, and the place where the priority filing was made, which had the country code US, or the United States. The dates indicate that it was filed nearly a year after the priority date in Britain, and published about six months after that, in accordance with normal procedure.

Below the priority data is given the name and address of the applicant in code (71). The inventor's address is not given. The difference between the inventor and the applicant is that it is the latter who intends to "work" the invention. Code (74) gives the name of the patent agent.

The subject classification details given by the Patent Office are on the right hand side. Code (51) gives the International Patent Classification (IPC) number, the superscript [7] showing that the seventh edition was used to classify the patent. Code (52) gives the British classification. Britain and the United States are the only major countries to use national classifications as well as the IPC.

Code (56) gives a brief search report. In this case four patents were found to be relevant. Code (58) tells us what was searched: British classification heading E1F FFG plus E21B 10/22 in the IPC. Sometimes as here online databases are mentioned as having been used in the search. The examiners will normally go back 50 years in the search.

In the bottom half of the page there is a title and an abstract, both provided by the applicant, and (if relevant) a representative drawing.

After the front page come the illustrations, introductory material, the description of the invention, and then the claims. From 1 April 1992 onwards the final pages consist of the detailed search report, in a similar format to that shown in Figure 3.4.

Figure 4.3 shows the front page of a granted, or B specification, GB 2 342 720 B. The arrangement of the information is somewhat different from that on the A document, and no abstract or drawing is given. The brief search report as in the A specification is given on the front page but the full report is not reproduced. The claims in the B document are the definitive monopoly given to the applicant.

C specifications are amendments to B specifications. They do not contain the revised text of the entire specification.

The A applications plus the old specifications (but not the B or C documents) are available on the Internet, notably at the free **Esp@cenet** site, from 1920 (there seem to be some gaps) as Adobe Acrobat documents.

(12) **UK Patent** (19) **GB** (11) **2 342 720** (13) **B**

(54) Title of Invention

A seat load measuring apparatus

(51) INT CL⁷; G01L 1/22, B60R 21/00

(21)	Application No **9924387.5**	(72)	Inventor(s) **Hiroshi Aoki**
(22)	Date of filing **15.10.1999**	(73)	Proprietor(s) **Takata Corporation**
(30)	Priority Data		**(Incorporated in Japan)**
	(31) **10294112**		**658 Echigawa**
	(32) **15.10.1998**		**Echigawa-cho** **Echi-gun Shiga 529-1338**
	(33) **JP**		**Japan**
(43)	Application published **19.04.2000**	(74)	Agent and/or Address for Service **James G Morgan**
(45)	Patent published **13.06.2001**		**31 Carlton Hill** **London** **NW8 0JX** **United Kingdom**
(52)	Domestic classification (Edition S) **G1N NAHS N1A3C1 N1F** **N3S11** **U1S S1142**		
(56)	Documents cited **GB2250345 A** **GB2221039 A** **EP0721099 A2** **WO98/22920 A1** **US5810392 A** **US5413378 A**		
(58)	Field of search As for published application 2342720 A *viz:* UK CL(Edition R) **G1N** **NAGBR NAHAS NAHAT** **NAHS NAHT** INT CL⁷ **B60N 2/00, B60R** **21/00, G01L 1/22** Online: **WPI, JAPIO, EPODOC** updated as appropriate		

Figure 4.3. Front page of a British grant

Abstracts

Abstracts of published British patent specifications are available from the first patent in 1617 (some topics were not covered before 1855). They are arranged in four series, which all consist of subject volumes (which contain indexes by subject and by name) with the abstracts in numerical order in each volume. From the second series (which began in 1855) they usually have an illustration. An exception is 1979-80, when the abstracts were arranged within the subject volumes in order of the headings ("subclasses").

Before the 1977 Patent Act the summaries, called abridgments, were prepared by Patent Office examiners. Since then the full front pages, including abstracts prepared by the applicants, are supplied. The Patent Office still has the power to amend unhelpful abstracts before publication.

The most recent series dates from 1962 onwards. Each week the front pages of published patent applications, arranged numerically within British classification divisions, are issued. Published volumes are substituted for them a couple of years later. These volumes contain cumulated annual subject-matter indexes.

An abstract for a particular specification can be identified by using the Divisional Allotment Index (formerly the Group Allotment Index). These numerical listings refer to the relevant subject volume. They commence with British patent 340,001, published in 1931.

It must be remembered that the increasing number of European Patent Convention and Patent Cooperation Treaty specifications since 1978 means that making a search through these British indexes is no longer comprehensive. This is because the other published applications have as much potential relevance for prior art and infringement purposes.

The *Europe Access* compact disk includes British title and other bibliographic data (including British classification) for patent specifications published since 1978 as well as data from several other countries. Otherwise some of the abridgments from 1920 are available on the free **Esp@cenet** database. Because the examiners prepared the earlier abridgments (those numbered below GB 2,000,000) they are considered valuable in keyword searching.

The gazette

The Patent Office's gazette, formerly called the *Official Journal (Patents)* or OJ(P) but from 5 February 1997 the *Patents and Designs Journal*, was formerly heavily used for current awareness searching. It can still be valuable for that (especially for filed applications which in this journal can only be searched by applicant) but the lack of abridgments hinders its use, and most subject searching is now done by using other sources such as the Internet.

The *Journal* first announces patent applications about six weeks after their submission to the Patent Office. Figure 4.4 gives an example of the information given, which is in alphabetical order of applicant with inventors being ignored (unless they are also applicants). The Elec Vision application, for example, had the title "Method for image positioning of a digital image capturing device". It was given the application number 0113997.1 when it was "lodged" or applied for on 8 June 2001. It was originally applied for in Taiwan (TW) on 25 August 2000, where it was given the application number 89117301.

1 August 2001   **Patents and Designs Journal No. 5855**   **2991**

Applications for Patents - cont

Ebbrell, Keith Rail bearing monitoring
Date Lodged: 08 Jun 2001
GB0113975.7

Elam, David M Shed locking system
Date Lodged: 07 Jun 2001
GB0113836.1

Electronic Data Holdings Limited
Hand-held data manager
Date Lodged: 07 Jun 2001
GB0113864.3

ElecVision Inc Method for image
positioning of a digital image capturing
device
Date Lodged: 08 Jun 2001
Priorities: [TW89117301 25 Aug 2000]
GB0113997.1

EMC Corporation Method and
apparatus for balancing workloads
among paths in a multi-path computer
system
Date Lodged: 08 Jun 2001 [29 Dec
1999]
PCT Appl No: PCT/US99/31105
PCT Pubn No: WO00/39679
Priorities: [US09223998 31 Dec 1998]
GB0114064.9

Engineering Business, The Limited
Improvements to cable ships
Date Lodged: 12 Jun 2001
Priorities: [GB0014188 12 Jun 2000]
GB0114270.2

Environmental Seals Limited
Apparatus for relieving the symptoms
of deep vein thrombosis
Date Lodged: 11 Jun 2001
GB0114027.6

Epoint Limited Drawer support
mechanism
Date Lodged: 12 Jun 2001
GB0114211.6

Ever Ready Limited Method of making
cathodes
Date Lodged: 08 Jun 2001
GB0113988.0

— Optimised alkaline electrochemical
cells
Date Lodged: 08 Jun 2001
GB0113990.6

— Optimised alkaline electrochemical
cells
Date Lodged: 08 Jun 2001
GB0113991.4

Eveready Battery Company Inc
Separator for electrochemical cells
Date Lodged: 08 Jun 2001
GB0113989.8

**ExxonMobil Upstream Research
Company** Ultra-high strength triple
phase steels with excellent cryogenic
tempreature toughness
Date Lodged: 08 Jun 2001 [16 Dec
1999]
PCT Appl No: PCT/US99/29804
PCT Pubn No: WO00/37689
Priorities: [US09215772 19 Dec 1998]
GB0114058.1

— Ultra-high strength ausaged steels with
excellent cryogenic temperature
toughness
Date Lodged: 08 Jun 2001 [16 Dec
1999]
PCT Appl No: PCT/US99/30055
PCT Pubn No: WO00/40764
[US09215773 19 Dec 1998]
GB0114062.3

F Hoffmann-La Roche AG Nucleoside
Derivatives
Date Lodged: 12 Jun 2001
GB0114286.8

Falmer Investments Limited Sealing
device
Date Lodged: 07 Jun 2001
GB0113925.2

Fast Technology AG Disc magnetic
torque sensing
Date Lodged: 12 Jun 2001
GB0114279.3

Fehrer, Monika A method and apparatus
for producing mop trimmings
Date Lodged: 11 Jun 2001
Priorities: [ATA10162000 13 Jun 2000]
GB0114148.0

Fentem, Andrew Computer-controlled
game board
Date Lodged: 08 Jun 2001
GB0113969.0

Fisher-Rosemount Systems, Inc.
Adaptiver predictive model in a process
control system
Date Lodged: 08 Jun 2001
Priorities: [US09590630 08 Jun 2000]
GB0113932.8

Fisher, Clive J Door system 2000/02
Flood protection barrier system
Date Lodged: 08 Jun 2001
GB0113954.2

— Protection door opening barrier system
2000/03
Date Lodged: 08 Jun 2001
GB0113955.9

Flamerite Fires Limited Apparatus for
simulating a flickering flame effect
Date Lodged: 08 Jun 2001
GB0113958.3

Ford Global Technologies, Inc. A motor
vehicle and an air distribution system
therefor
Date Lodged: 08 Jun 2001
GB0113957.5

Formosa Electronic Industries Inc
Multi-functional power adapter with
dual plug structure
Date Lodged: 09 Jun 2001
GB0114063.1

Formway Furniture Limited A work
station support and/or a mounting
bracket used in said work station
support
Date Lodged: 11 Jun 2001 [22 Jun 1998]
Priorities: [NZ328194 26 Jun 1997]
GB0114206.6

Forrest, Fred Collapsible metal container
Date Lodged: 11 Jun 2001
GB0114163.9

Forschungszentrum Jülich GmbH A
removal apparatus for removing
spherical fuel element pellets and a
method of removing fuel element
pellets from nuclear reactors
Date Lodged: 07 Jun 2001
Priorities: [DE10029145 14 Jun 2000]
GB0113903.9

Foster, D P Faster connection leads
Date Lodged: 12 Jun 2001
GB0114220.7

Fox, John Clamp and cur board
Date Lodged: 09 Jun 2001 [23 May
2000]
GB0114121.7

Freeline Communications Limited
Apparatus for playing a game and a
method of providing a game
Date Lodged: 12 Jun 2001
GB0114241.3

Fujitsu Limited System and method for
continuous delivery schedule including
automated customernotification
Date Lodged: 08 Jun 2001
Priorities: [US09684859 05 Oct 2000]
GB0114021.9

G.T.W. Developments Ltd Pneumatic
yarn splicer
Date Lodged: 11 Jun 2001
GB0114065.6

Gang, Qin A computer monitor joins a
liquid tank
Date Lodged: 08 Jun 2001
GB0114001.1

Garth, Peter Treatment of lithographic
printing plates
Date Lodged: 12 Jun 2001
GB0114186.0

Gee, David H Door opening and closing
mechanism for a motor vehicle
Date Lodged: 13 Jun 2001
GB0114315.5

General Domestic Appliances Limited
Gas cooking appliance
Date Lodged: 08 Jun 2001
Priorities: [GB0013861 08 Jun 2000]
GB0113973.2

Figure 4.4. Filed applications listed in the Patents and Designs Journal

The advantages of being given the priority information are that it indicates the novelty date for examination purposes, and suggests that publication will occur up to a year earlier than domestic priority applications, since this is normally 18 months after the earliest date given in the entry. The priority data can also assist searching for other members of the patent family. The following EMC entry indicates that it was originally filed in the USA and was then published in the PCT system as WO00/39679, and that a British patent is being requested. The date in brackets in the "date lodged" field is the filing date in the PCT system. The priority may be British as in the General Domestic Appliances entry. This is the novelty date and again publication will be 18 months from that date.

When the applications are published, brief details are given in the *Journal* in British abbreviated (British) classified order. An example is given in Figure 4.5. Since the applications are arranged in classified order before they are numbered, this forms a numerical sequence as well. The British classification is roughly similar in its arrangement to the International Patent Classification so someone familiar with that system can use either the *Journal* or the actual published applications for current awareness scanning. References are given from subordinate to the more important subject aspects of a patent application. For example, there is a reference from A5E to A5G for GB 2358586, where the full entry is given.

The information given for that same GB 2358586 is as follows. The filing number, GB 0002124.6, has after it the date of filing of the application, 31 January 2000. The applicant's name is given, and the title, "Air freshener or insecticide composition". Any priority details are given. These are usually foreign but can refer to earlier attempts to file in Britain where a mistake meant that re-filing was required (with the original date being used for priority), as in the next entry, GB 2358587. All the relevant British classification headings are given plus a U1S meaning that an extra class allowing for a functional aspect not indexed by the classification has been provided, followed by the "Int Cl^7" numbers. These are the classification numbers of the latest, 7th edition of the International Patent Classification.

The published applications are indexed by applicant in each issue of the *Journal*, as shown in Figure 4.6. There are references from the inventors to their companies, as for Steven Ring to Wireless Systems International. Within each firm the inventors' names are given in brackets by order of published number (and hence within a British classified sequence, as in Reckitt Benckiser's case). These indexes are cumulated annually into published volumes.

Similar bibliographic details are given for granted patents which are indexed by subject and by applicant. There are no published cumulative indexes for granted patents.

Patent Cooperation Treaty applications designating Britain

It is possible to designate Britain in the published Patent Cooperation Treaty (PCT) applications to indicate that a national patent is wanted at grant. This can either be through a national British patent or through a European Patent Convention application. In both cases the relevant patent office allocates a number from its A publication sequence, typically 8 months after publication of the PCT specification. The British Patent Office only prints front pages if the PCT application were published in English, indicating

CHAPTER 4: THE BRITISH PATENT SYSTEM

Applications published: Subject-Matter Index - cont

Priorities: [AUPP7162 17 Nov 1998]

PCT Details: PCT/AU99/01016
WO00/28836 25 May 2000

UKC Headings: A2B *Int Cl*^{7} A23L 1/10
A23L 1/164

A3H

GB2358574 (GB0001837.4) 26 Jan 2000
LUEN TAT WATCH BAND
MANUFACTURING LIMITED
(INCORPORATED IN HONG
KONG)
Insertable gemstone setting

UKC Headings: A3H *Int Cl*^{7} A44C 17/04

A3V

GB2358575 (GB0001884.6) 28 Jan 2000
SMITH, NIEL C
A cycle helmet with integral front and rear
lamps

UKC Headings: A3V *Int Cl*^{7} A42B 3/04

A4A

GB2358576 (GB0001906.7) 27 Jan 2000
OTTER CONTROLS LIMITED
(INCORPORATED IN THE UNITED
KINGDOM)
Control of liquid boiling appliance

UKC Headings: A4A *Int Cl*^{7} A47J 27/21

A4B

GB2358577 (GB9914104.6) 17 Jun 1999
JOHNSTON, ALLAN
Fence post bracket for hanging baskets

UKC Headings: A4B *Int Cl*^{7} A47G 7/04

A4F

GB2358578 (GB0111741.5) 14 May 2001
[03 Nov 1999]
MIRANDA, HENRY R
Bath system for semiconductor wafers
with obliquely mounted sonic transducers

Priorities: [US9192148 14 Nov 1998]

PCT Details: PCT/US99/25874
WO00/29135 25 May 2000

UKC Headings: A4F H1K *Int Cl*^{7} B08B
3/12

GB2358579 (GB0112949.3) 29 May 2001
[06 May 1998]
HOOVER, THE COMPANY
(INCORPORATED IN USA -
DELAWARE)
Vacuum cleaner suction nozzle
configuration
Divisional earlier date under section 15 (4)
GB9809641.5
Priorities: [US08/853838 09 May 1997]
UKC Headings: A4F *Int Cl*^{7} A47L 9/04

A4L

GB2358580 (GB0022015.2) 08 Sep 2000
[11 Mar 1999]
LEEC LIMITED (INCORPORATED
IN THE UNITED KINGDOM)
A down draught autopsy table
Priorities: [GB9805048 11 Mar 1998]
PCT Details: PCT/GB99/00750
WO99/45881 16 Sep 1999

UKC Headings: A4L *Int Cl*^{7} A61G 13/00

GB2358581 (GB0101890.2) 24 Jan 2001
KDB ENGINEERING PTY LTD
(INCORPORATED IN AUSTRALIA)
Wear indicating ferrule tip containing a
cavity
Priorities: [AUPQ5275 25 Jan 2000]

UKC Headings: A4L *Int Cl*^{7} A47B 91/04

A4P

GB2358663 *See* entry under Heading E2A

A5B

GB2358582 (GB0019028.0) 04 Aug 2000
ASTRAZENECA AB
(INCORPORATED IN SWEDEN)
Stabilised pharmaceutical compositions
Priorities: [GB0001621 26 Jan 2000]

UKC Headings: A5B U1S *Int Cl*^{7} A61K
31/506 A61K 31/505 A61P 3/06 A61P 9/
10

GB2358583 (GB0019029.8) 04 Aug 2000
ASTRAZENECA AB
(INCORPORATED IN SWEDEN)
Stabilised pharmaceutical compositions
Priorities: [GB0001621 26 Jan 2000]
UKC Headings: A5B U1S *Int Cl*^{7} A61K
31/506 A61K 31/505 A61P 3/06 A61P 9/
10

GB2358584 (GB0029455.3) 04 Dec 2000
SMITHKLINE BEECHAM P.L.C.
(INCORPORATED IN THE UNITED
KINGDOM)
Oral care composition
Priorities: [GB9930569 23 Dec 1999]
UKC Headings: A5B U1S *Int Cl*^{7} A61K
7/16

A5E

GB2358585 (GB0027657.6) 13 Nov 2000
MICROTEK CORPORATION SA
(INCORPORATED IN
SWITZERLAND)
Pesticidal composition also comprising a
substance which tastes unpleasant to the
animal to which the composition is to be
applied

Priorities: [GB9926699 12 Nov 1999]

UKC Headings: A5E U1S *Int Cl*^{7} A01N
25/32 A01N 25/00 A01N 25/32 A01N
39:00 A01N 53:08 A01N 25/00 A01N
39:00 A01N 53:08

GB2358586 *See* entry under Heading A5G

A5G

GB2358586 (GB0002124.6) 31 Jan 2000
RECKITT BENCKISER (UK)
LIMITED (INCORPORATED IN
THE UNITED KINGDOM)
Air freshener or insecticide composition

UKC Headings: A5G A5E U1S *Int Cl*^{7}
A61L 9/01 A01N 25/02

GB2358587 (GB0025785.7) 20 Oct 2000
WAGHORN, FREDERICK F
Aroma dispenser with coiled absorbent
layer

Priorities: [GB9924968 21 Oct 1999]

UKC Headings: A5G *Int Cl*^{7} A61L 9/03
A61L 9/12

A5R

GB2358588 (GB0001503.2) 25 Jan 2000
WINSTONE, SAMANTHA K
Feminine hygiene pad

UKC Headings: A5R *Int Cl*^{7} A61F 13/472
A61F 13/476

GB2358589 (GB0111074.1) 04 May 2001
[10 Jul 1998]
WARDLAW, DOUGLAS
Valve structure

Divisional earlier date under section 15 (4)
GB0000208.9

Priorities: [GB9714580.9 10 Jul 1997]

UKC Headings: A5R *Int Cl*^{7} A61F 2/44

GB2358663 *See* entry under Heading E2A

GB2358752 *See* entry under Heading H4F

Figure 4.5. Published applications listed by subject in the Patents and Designs Journal

3024   Patents and Designs Journal No. 5855   1 August 2001

Applications published: Name Index - cont

Oddy, Doug *See* Mitel Corporation (Incorporated in Canada - Ontario)

Oinonen, Olli *See* Robotic Technology Systems Plc (Incorporated in the United Kingdom)

Okano, Taichi *See* Showa Denko K K (Incorporated in Japan)

Ollis, Mark *See* Carnegie Mellon University (Incorporated in USA - Pennsylvania)

Olthof, Henricus J B *See* Ventilatoren Sirocco Howden BV (Incorporated in the Netherlands)

Ontario Drive & Gear Limited (Incorporated in Canada) (Szymkowiak, Zbigniew) F2D GB2358681

Origin Technologies Limited (Incorporated in the United Kingdom) (Groves, Mark D) (Rock, Timothy M) H4D B7H G4Q GB2358749 (Groves, Mark D) (Rock, Timothy M) H4D B7H G4Q GB2358750

Otter Controls Limited (Incorporated in the United Kingdom) (Smith, David A) (Walford, Mark J) A4A GB2358576

Paice, Shaun *See* 3Com Corporation (Incorporated in USA - California)

Palmer, Graham F *See* eLlist Ltd (Incorporated in the United Kingdom)

Park, Jin-Young *See* Samsung Electronics Company Limited (Incorporated in the Republic of Korea)

Parsons, Mark J *See* Russell Roof Tiles Limited (Incorporated in the United Kingdom)

Parsons, Ronald E B4W GB2358605

Patel, Dinesh R *See* Schlumberger Technology Corporation (Incorporated in USA - Texas)

Payne, Bernard J G5R H4F U1S GB2358729

Penny, Richard S *See* Aspect Vision Care Ltd. (Incorporated in the United Kingdom)

Perle, Andrew *See* Madison Research (Incorporated in Ireland)

Pferdmenges, Gerd *See* Trützschler GmbH & Co. KG (Incorporated in the Federal Republic of Germany)

Picard, Francois *See* Sagem SA (Incorporated in France)

PII Limited (Incorporated in the United Kingdom) (Couchman, Peter A) (Maughan, David C) F2P GB2358689 (Couchman, Peter A) (Easton, Eric) (Houldey, Peter) (Maughan, David C) F2P GB2358690

Pike, Brian C *See* Bradman Lake Limited (Incorporated in the United Kingdom)

Pinard, Debbie *See* Mitel Corporation (Incorporated in Canada - Ontario)

Ping, Gong H *See* Ross, Finlay M T

Pipeline Induction Heat Limited (Incorporated in the United Kingdom) (Cottrell, Terrence) (Daykin, Damian) B3D GB2358601

Pirkola, Jani *See* Nokia Mobile Phones Limited (Incorporated in Finland)

Plaskett, Allan H4F H4R U1S GB2358755

Pollard, Andrew *See* GKN Automotive GmbH (Incorporated in the Federal Republic of Germany)

Posch, Andreas *See* LuK Lamellen und Kupplungsbau GmbH (Incorporated in the Federal Republic of Germany)

Project Leisure Limited (Incorporated in the United Kingdom) (Boulton, Anthony D) A6H GB2358591

Reckitt Benckiser (UK) Limited (Incorporated in the United Kingdom) (Lang, Angus) A5G A5E U1S GB2358586 (Fox, Rodney T) (Harper, Duncan R) C5D GB2358638 (Bedford, David) (Braithwaite, Jean) C5D GB2358639

Reid, Ewan G L *See* Balmoral Group Limited (Incorporated in the United Kingdom)

Riken Keiki Co., Ltd (Incorporated in Japan) (Imaya, Hiroshi) (Matsuda, Hiroyuki) G1N U1S GB2358707

Ring, Steven R *See* Wireless Systems International Limited (Incorporated in the United Kingdom)

Risen, William *See* Spalding Sports Worldwide Inc (Incorporated in USA - Massachusetts)

Roberts, Douglas J *See* Gerber Coburn Optical Inc (Incorporated in USA - Connecticut)

Roberts, George A F *See* BTG International Limited (Incorporated in the United Kingdom)

Roberts, Mark A and Biggs, William P B7D B7J GB2358618

Robotic Technology Systems Plc (Incorporated in the United Kingdom) (Leppäjärvi, Seppo O A) (Oinonen, Olli) G1A GB2358702

Roby, Mary D *See* Lucent Technologies Inc (Incorporated in USA - Delaware)

Rock, Timothy M *See* Origin Technologies Limited (Incorporated in the United Kingdom)

Rodriguez, Herman *See* International Business Machines Corporation (Incorporated in USA - New York)

Roke Manor Research Limited (Incorporated in the United Kingdom) (Hancock, Robert) (McCann, Stephen) (West, Mark A) H4P GB2358776

Rolls-Royce plc (Incorporated in the United Kingdom) (Allen, John W) (Maguire, Alan R) F2A F1T GB2358678

Ross, Finlay M T (Ping, Gong H) F1F GB2358675

Ross, Gordon G4A GB2358717 H4T GB2358778

Round, Michael S *See* Yale Security Products UK Limited (Incorporated in the United Kingdom)

Routliffe, Stephen G *See* Mitel Corporation (Incorporated in Canada - Ontario)

Rudolphi, Norbert *See* LuK Lamellen und Kupplungsbau GmbH (Incorporated in the Federal Republic of Germany)

Rumford, Peter *See* Bericap UK Limited (Incorporated in the United Kingdom)

Rushworth, Simon A *See* Epichem Limited (Incorporated in the United Kingdom)

Russell Roof Tiles Limited (Incorporated in the United Kingdom) (Barker, Howard A) (Freathy, Paul) (Parsons, Mark J) E1D GB2358649

Safeguard Site Security Fencing Limited (Incorporated in the United Kingdom) (Issott, John L) E1D GB2358646

Sagem SA (Incorporated in France) (Picard, Francois) H4F GB2358754

Salomaki, Lauri *See* Nokia Mobile Phones Limited (Incorporated in Finland)

Samsung Electronics Company Limited (Incorporated in the Republic of Korea) (Kim, Heon-Cheol) (Park, Jin-Young) G4A GB2358721 (Chen, Shiao-Hua) (Koo, Ja C) (Kwon, Hae S) G5R GB2358730 (Jeon, Jong-gu) H4P GB2358775

Saunders, Stephen *See* Aspect Vision Care Ltd. (Incorporated in the United Kingdom)

Schlumberger Technology Corporation (Incorporated in USA - Texas) (Patel, Dinesh R) E1F GB2358656

Figure 4.6. Published applications listed by name in the Patents and Designs Journal

that it is a PCT document. If the PCT were not published in English then a translation of the entire specification is published instead. In 1999 1,265 PCT applications entered the national phase in Britain, that is, a request was made that a British patent be granted.

Britain and the European Patent Convention

Besides providing information on British patents published through the Patent Office, the *Journal* also covers those European Patent Convention patents that designate Britain, since they are also national patents. They are called "European Patents (UK)".

This information consists of listings of granted patents, with applicant but not title, and "Non-English" if the patent is in a foreign language; listings of translations of European granted patents, and of claims of applications; European patents treated as void due to failure to file translations; revoked patents; and European patents that have ceased in Britain through non payment of renewal fees.

From 1987 European Patent Convention granted patents that were published in French or German but which designate Britain must be translated in order to be valid patents in Britain. The translation consists of the description plus the claims (which would have been translated anyway in the original grant). Both the Patent Office and the British Library keep paper sets of these translations.

Some British applicants routinely abandon a British application and continue with the European Patent Convention equivalent. Others allow both applications to run through to grant. However, if both are granted the Patent Office will insist on the British patent being revoked. Alternatively the British designation in the European specification may have been dropped.

Case law

British law involves specialist courts for intellectual property. No juries are used and a judge or examiner (acting on behalf of the Comptroller General of the Patent Office) makes the decisions. Traditionally the civil courts interpreted the wording of the claims literally but since the Catnic decision (in 1982) a more relaxed interpretation of the wording has been used. The patent court cases can be divided into two main kinds: Patent Office Court decisions, and various Court decisions.

Patent Office decisions are either hearings before a Patent Office senior examiner when an application for an industrial property right has been refused, or can be used as a cheap way of settling disputes (often on licensing). They cannot be cited as precedents in other courts.

On appeal, cases from both the Patent Office and the County Patent Court can go on to the High Court. Cases can also begin in the Chancery Division of the High Court. Alternatively they can begin in a new Patents County Court which has been operating since 1990. After the Court of Appeal, cases can eventually go on appeal to the House of Lords. All these courts are in London.

The British Library holds transcripts of many intellectual property decisions given after hearings in the British courts from 1970 onwards. Many of them are never formally published. They are separated into the O series for Patent Office decisions and the C series for High Court, Patents County Court and House of Lord decisions.

These series ought to be complete except for the High Court series, of which a selection only is held. There may be copyright restrictions on some of the C series.

Card indexes of the parties involved in both series from 1976 are available at the British Library. The Court Service Judgments Database at **http://www.courtservice.gov.uk/ judgments/judg_frame.htm** holds copies of High Court and Court of Appeal cases from about the middle of 1998. Some free information is held at the Smith Bernal International website, **http://www.smithbernal.com**.

The Patent Office's patent information services

Besides examining and granting patents, the British Patent Office offers both publications and services. Many of these are listed (with current prices) on the back page of each issue of the *Journal*, and details of many services provided by the Patent Office are also given.

These services include supplying copies of British patents, and translations of European-granted patents. There is also a current awareness service whereby either lists of patent numbers, or actual specifications, within British classification profiles can be provided. These services are dealt with by the Patent Sales Branch whose contact details are:

The Patent Office, Concept House, Cardiff Road, Newport, Gwent NP10 8QQ, UK.
Tel: +44 (0) 1633 813651.
Fax: +44 (0) 1633 814444.

It is possible to obtain information such as name and address of proprietor; confirmation of the status of a patent; to whom a patent is being licensed; and to obtain copies of the file of correspondence relating to a published patent application. The Patent Office can be contacted on their central enquiry number, 08459 500 505 or on email enquiries@patent.gov.uk for details on how to use these services.

The Patent Office also contains the Search and Advisory Service. This offers a comprehensive range of online patents databases. It also has access to specialist patent examiners who can offer expert search services, and a large classified set of patent documents and provide comments on novelty etc. Their contact details are:

Search and Advisory Service, The Patent Office, Concept House, Cardiff Road, Newport, Gwent, NP10 8QQ, UK
Telephone: +44 (0) 1633 811010
Fax: +44 (0) 1633 811020
Email: commercialsearches@patent.gov.uk

The British Library and the British patents

This section explains special practices at the British Library in making British patent information available.

The British applications published each week are numerically arranged on a table before being replaced by the following week's publications. Since the applications are published in British classified order it is easy to identify specifications on a particular topic.

The granted patents for the last three weeks are kept numerically in separate boxes for each week before shelving in the main sequence.

The British Library keeps recent British abstracts in boxes, arranged by subject group, for each year. Subject access is provided by a separate series of black binders containing weekly updates, each in classified sequence, of the specifications published that week.

There is a telephone at the British Patents Desk that can be used to talk to Patent Office examiners about how to classify a particular subject by British or International Patent Classification.

The filed applications cannot be searched by subject before they are published, other than online using the title information or by using the (priced) Delphion service at **http://www.delphion.com/**. However, searches by applicant can be carried out in annual cumulations, which are kept on card indexes at the British Library (the current year plus the four previous years are on open access). The information is exactly the same as in the *Journal*, but the cards are filed in the current cumulation about two weeks before the same information appears in the *Journal*.

The *Journal* is useful for current awareness but it can also be important to find the published numbers for an application that was noticed years earlier in the *Journal* or online, or to find out what subsequently happened to a published application. In practice this is now normally done by consulting the official Patent Status Enquiry database at **http://webdb4.patent.gov.uk/patents** which is searchable by filing or published number for British or EP (UK) grants. Detailed information is confined to published specifications (but brief details are given of filings as reported in the *Journal*). The information varies but can be very full, such as giving change of ownership, extension of protection, and so on as well as status information. An example is given in Figure 4.7. The British Library maintains two sets of non-official registers, which are compiled by using information given in the *Journal*. They are updated as soon as the *Journal* is published. They give less data than the database.

The first of these is the **Application Register**. This gives the published number for every application number or, if it were not published, the outcome of the application. Some are indicated as having "terminated" before publication. Others needed to be submitted more than once, and a stamp is given showing earlier or later applications. Those published applications that were withdrawn before grant are shown as such. Until 1996 we attempted through routine scanning of various journals, to give foreign equivalents, and especially for EP equivalents for British filings.

The second set of registers is the **Stages of Progress Register**. This explains what happens to published applications, giving the dates of the published *Journal* issues which give the data (which may be weeks after the event has occurred). Some are withdrawn before grant; some are "no case", where a number was incorrectly assigned; and some are granted. If nothing has happened the case is said to be pending. If the patent lapses due to non-payment of renewal fees, which are due annually from five years after application, this is recorded. It is possible to restore apparently lapsed patents under certain conditions so this information should be treated with caution. The date of the *Journal* reporting that a patent has run its full term and expired is also given.

The "Remarks" column can contain many different comments on status changes. One of these is a red "L of R" or if in an old register an asterisk. This indicates that the owner of the patent has declared a licence of right, by which in exchange for only paying half the renewal fees, the invention is licensed to any interested party on a non-exclusive basis. A licence of right can also be imposed on the owner of patents if the patent is not "worked".

Internet databases

The Patent Status database at **http://webdb4.patent.gov.uk/patents** provides current status information on both in force and pending British patents and on granted European patents which designate Britain. Those which have lost protection are also retained on the database. It is searchable by filing or published number. There is a separate SPC Search database at **http://webdb2.patent.gov.uk/rspc** which can be used to search for known British or EP (UK) patents which have had extra terms added to allow for waiting for permission to be marketed. An example is shown in Figure 4.7.

The **Esp@cenet** database at **http://gb.espacenet.com** includes a "Great Britain" file but this is only for the last two years. More useful is the "worldwide" file which can be searched for Britain alone by using <GB> in the publication number field. It can be searched by abstract words, applicant or IPC classification (or its variant ECLA) back to the late 1970s and to some extent back to 1920 (but there are some gaps). Links are usually present to Adobe Acrobat copies of the A (but not B) specifications.

The priced Delphion database at **http://www.delphion.com** provides legal status data. The Case Law section of this chapter lists free databases giving court cases.

The DEPATISnet database at **http://www.depatisnet.de** includes Adobe Acrobat copies of British A specifications from 1920 and allows some searching by other elements.

PATENTS STATUS INFORMATION

FULL DETAILS

Please click on button below to view the published patent application via esp@cenet.

ESP@CENET

REGISTER ENTRY FOR GB2223459

Form 1 Application No GB8922531.2 filing date 06.10.1989

Priority claimed:
    07.10.1988 in United Kingdom - doc: 8823586

Title COLLAPSIBLE BOAT

Applicant/Proprietor
    KEITH RAYMOND MATTHEWS, 49 Seamons Close, Dunstable, Bedfordshire, LU6,
    United Kingdom   [ADP No. 04386173001]

Inventor
    KEITH RAYMOND MATTHEWS, 49 Seamons Close, Dunstable, Bedfordshire, LU6,
    United Kingdom   [ADP No. 04386173001]

Classified to
    B7A
    B63B

Address for Service
    BOWLES HORTON, Felden House,Dower Mews, High Street, BERKHAMSTED, Herts,
    HP4 2BL, United Kingdom   [ADP No. 00008805003]

Publication No GB2223459 dated 11.04.1990

Examination requested 12.07.1990

Patent Granted with effect from 26.08.1992 (Section 25(1)) with title
    COLLAPSIBLE BOAT

04.05.1995 Patent ceased on 06.10.1994

        **** END OF REGISTER ENTRY ****

RENEWALS DATA

        Date Filed   06.10.1989

        Date Not in Force   06.10.1994

        Date of Last Renewal 24.09.1993

        Year of Last Renewal   5

Figure 4.7. British status data from the official database

Contact information

The Patent Office
Concept House
Tredegar Park
Cardiff Road
Newport, Gwent NP9 1RH
UK

Tel: (UK callers) 08459 500 505
Tel: (International callers) +44 1633 813930
Fax: +44 (0) 1633 813600
Email: enquiries@patent.gov.uk
Web address: **http://www.patent.gov.uk**

Further reading

A review of biotech patent cases: anarchy in the UK? P. Gilbert and A. Wilson, *Patent World*, 2001, 133, 24-26.

Economical with the articles (or, should programs be patentable?) M.G. Harman, *CIPA*, 2001, 30 (4), 193-197.

Patent litigation: past and future. R. Lawrence, *CIPA*, 2001, 30 (2), 89-92.

The enforcement of patents in the United Kingdom. W. Cornish, D. Llewelyn, *IIC*, 2001, 31 (6), 627-645.

5. THE UNITED STATES PATENT SYSTEM

In the year 2000 157,497 patents were granted in the USA. Of these 54% were of American origin. The leading foreign countries were 31,296 from Japan (or 19.8% of all patents), 10,234 from Germany (6.4%) and 4,667 from Taiwan (2.9%). In 1995 only 101,419 patents were granted. Reasons for the steep increase are arguable but these must include newly patentable fields in biology and software.

Numeration and document codes

When a patent application is made at the American Patent and Trademark Office (USPTO) it is allocated an application or "serial" number. These numbers are allocated in sequences from 1 to under 1,000,000, with the number reverting to 1 in the year when the numbers seem likely to go over 1,000,000. They are sometimes also referred to by the series of such numbers that they belong to. The ninth series began in 1998 and filings may be called e.g. 09/200,000 instead of just 200,000. The seventh series began in 1987 and the eighth in 1993. These filing numbers can cause confusion both because it is not certain which series is meant, and because often they are cited as if they were publication numbers, e.g. "US 200,000". Since US 1,000,000 was published in 1911, any cited patent with a lower number is clearly going to be older. More details would be required to identify it as a search would have to be made for any published specifications sharing that filing number in order to identify the correct one. Often the year of filing, or the subject, or the applicant is known which will assist identification. These application numbers are given at INID code (21) on the front page of both series of published specifications.

Since 8 June 1995 it has been possible to file a provisional patent application. They are used to gain extra priority as explained in the next section. Provisionals are numbered in a series beginning with 60/000001 and can be used in the same INID code (21) as regular filing numbers (although they cannot be confused with them as the numbers are so different). Use of these numbers has been confused in published specifications and sometimes they are used in the priority area and sometimes not.

Until the passing of the American Inventor's Protection Act of 1999 applications in the American system were only published if they were "issued" or granted. Under the Act applications made on or after 29 November 2000 must be published 18 months from the priority date as a Patent Application Publication unless there is no intention to file abroad. A statement is filed which can later be withdrawn, allowing publication, without penalty. This exception (unique in the world) means that many inventions by small companies or private inventors are exempt. The first of these applications was published on 15 March 2001 and was numbered in the format 2001/0000001 A1 onwards. A reprinted application will be coded A2 and a further correction A9. It is anticipated that about 180,000 will be published annually when the system is in full operation.

Otherwise American patent specifications have only been published at grant. Those before 1836 were not numbered. In 1836 the specifications began to be numbered in a sequence beginning with 1. The first patent to be published in 2001 was numbered 6,167,569. From January 2001 these granted patents acquired for the first time a document code, B1, but B2 will be used instead for those that were previously published as an application within the US system. B8 is the code for a corrected front page and B9 for a corrected complete specification.

Patenting procedure

The USA often calls patent specifications for inventions "utility" patents to distinguish them from other types such as "design" patents. The use by the USPTO of the word "patents" normally means that they are all included. This section is about "utility" patents only.

Patent applicants to the USA have to fill in an "invention disclosure" indicating relevant prior art, and often such information is also given in the opening pages of the description. These disclosures are supposed to avoid "fraud on the patent office" where applicants deliberately mislead the examiners as to the novelty of the invention. The USA is now alone in establishing novelty by the date of invention rather than that of filing. This leads to carefully documented notebooks in American research establishments which show when an invention was first thought of. It is now open to foreigners to use such notebooks as evidence in US courts of when an idea was thought of. If two applications are filed on similar subjects then an "interference" is called and the parties are asked to provide evidence on when they made the invention.

Since 8 June 1995 it has been possible to file a provisional patent application. This can be altered and refiled within 12 months as a regular patent application, and subsequent filing abroad under the Paris Convention can occur within 12 months of that later date. Patent terms only run from the regular application date but priority runs from the provisional date if quoted.

American patents can also be modified while pending by adding further novel information. These are reflected by "Related U.S. Application Data" on the front pages of published applications or grants, which sometimes refer to previously published specifications, and which usually refer to "divisions" of earlier applications.

The inventor, or "patentee", is considered to be the owner of the intellectual property in the invention, and is prominently named at top left on the front page. The "assignee" at INID code (73) of the grant is the actual applicant and will be a company or other organisation, or an individual, to whom the rights have been assigned. This occurs even if the inventor (or "assignor") works for the assignee.

American patents were formerly published only when granted. This made foreign publications which were published 18 months from priority (such as PCT specifications) of the invention a valuable source of information. Since 29 November 2000 any filed patent applications must be published 18 months from priority unless the applicant does not intend to file abroad. The first of these was published on 15 March 2001. These specifications often lack an applicant (or "assignee", the usual American term) and do not have search reports. They are published on Thursdays but only in electronic format. A PDF version is available on the database at the official Patent Full-Text and Full-Page

Image Databases at **http://www.uspto.gov/patft/index.html**. The name of the site reflects both that the actual text is available to search by keyword or within front page details, and that the images (including any drawings) are available. There are other non-official sites that also host American images or material such as **Esp@cenet**.

The average delay until "disposal" (rejecting or granting a patent) is now said to be 20 months. Applications concerning biological or electronic topics are likely to be much more delayed. Until the new publication system (which does not cover all applications) "submarine" patents could suddenly emerge many years after filing and businesses that would be affected by them would have to respond rapidly. Granted or "issued" patents are published on Tuesdays although now they are only available electronically.

From the 1980s the Patent Office has begun to allow the patenting of an increasing range of technologies. These include microorganisms, DNA, algorithms, and business methods. Some areas are only patentable in the USA and generally the USA leads the way in opening up patenting in new areas.

Until 1980 patents could never lapse (as opposed to expire) from protection as no "maintenance" or renewal fees were paid. Patents which were applied for after 12 December 1980 must have maintenance fees paid at intervals of $3\frac{1}{2}$, $7\frac{1}{2}$ and $11\frac{1}{2}$ years after grant. There is no compulsion to make the applicant "work" the invention. Patents were formerly protected for 17 years from the date of grant. As of 8 June 1995 patents granted or pending as of that date received 20 years' protection from the earliest date of domestic filing on the patent, or 17 years from grant, whichever was longer. Applications filed from that date received 20 years from the earliest regular filing date subject to maintenance fees being paid.

Patent terms can be extended to allow for waiting for permission to market a product. This affects pharmaceuticals. There are various sites giving information on this listed under US at the British Library site **http://www.bl.uk/services/information/patents/othlink2.html#sub**.

Specifications

From the beginning of 2000 only electronic formats were used to publish American specifications.

The prior art, description and drawings in an American patent are often more detailed than in similar patents abroad. This is due to American legal requirements. Unlike the grants the published applications have the paragraphs in the descriptions coded [0001], [0002], etc.

An example of the front page of a patent application publication is given in Figure 5.1. The inventor's surname is prominently given at top left, Zhang. As here the company's name need not be given. Originally filed in Japan as long ago as 26 May 1993 (as shown in INID code (30)) it was repeatedly continued as an application or divided (code (60)) until filed on 1 December 2000 (code (22)) and given the application number 09/726,337. Besides the International Patent Classification (given in code (51)) the American national classification is given at code (52). Many prefer to use the American classification rather than the International to find American patents by class. This is partly

US 20010000011A1

(19) **United States**
(12) **Patent Application Publication** (10) Pub. No.: **US 2001/0000011 A1**
Zhang et al. (43) Pub. Date: **Mar. 15, 2001**

(54) **METHOD FOR PRODUCING SEMICONDUCTOR DEVICE**

(76) Inventors: **Hongyong Zhang**, Kanagawa (JP); **Toru Takayama**, Kanagawa (JP)

Correspondence Address:
NIXON PEABODY LLP
Suite 800
8180 Greensboro Drive
McLean, VA 22102 (US)

(21) Appl. No.: **09/726,337**

(22) Filed: **Dec. 1, 2000**

Related U.S. Application Data

(60) Division of application No. 09/122,664, filed on Jul. 27, 1998, Pat. No. 6,160,279, which is a division of application No. 08/715,770, filed on Sep. 19, 1996,

Pat. No. 5,830,784, which is a continuation of application No. 08/248,085, filed on May 24, 1994, now abandoned.

(30) **Foreign Application Priority Data**

May 26, 1993 (JP) 5-147005

Publication Classification

(51) Int. Cl.^{7} H01L 29/786
(52) U.S. Cl. 257/59; 257/347

(57) **ABSTRACT**

A silicon film provided on a blocking film **102** on a substrate **101** is made amorphous by doping Si+, and in a heat-annealing process, crystallization is started in parallel to a substrate from an area **100** where lead serving as a crystallization-promoting catalyst is introduced.

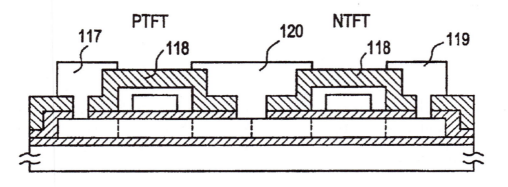

Figure 5.1. Front page of an American application

because the USPTO reclassifies all subjects as they go along so that there are correct file lists of all patents by class back to 1790, but mainly because the International classification is assigned by running the American classification through a computer concordance. This means that the International class is often not very precise or helpful.

The front page, description, and claims of a granted American patent, US 6,199,351 B1, is shown in Figure 5.2. The date of patent (that is, grant) is given at top right in INID code (45) as 13 March 2001. The inventor's surname, in this case Mount, is given at the top left. Only the town of the inventor (or patentee) and of the applicant (or assignee) must be given at codes (73) or (75), although full addresses are provided for "small entities" (private inventors or small companies). The application number for this patent is given in code (21) as 08/951,389. Before 13 April 1999 the series number, in this case 8, was omitted. "Related US application data" can appear in code (62). It can be helpful in linking up directly related material by citing filing or published numbers. Because of the nature of American patent laws many applications are split up in this way.

(12) United States Patent
Mount

(10) Patent No.: **US 6,199,351 B1**
(45) Date of Patent: ***Mar. 13, 2001**

(54) **PACKAGING MACHINE**

(75) Inventor: **Michael John Mount**, Middlesex (GB)

(73) Assignee: **Wright Machinery Limited**, Uxbridge (GB)

(*) Notice: This patent issued on a continued prosecution application filed under 37 CFR 1.53(d), and is subject to the twenty year patent term provisions of 35 U.S.C. 154(a)(2).

Subject to any disclaimer, the term of this patent is extended or adjusted under 35 U.S.C. 154(b) by 0 days.

(21) Appl. No.: **08/951,389**

(22) Filed: **Oct. 16, 1997**

(30) **Foreign Application Priority Data**

Oct. 16, 1996 (GB) 9621609

(51) Int. Cl.^{7} **B65B 1/02**
(52) U.S. Cl. **53/563; 53/570; 53/386.1**
(58) Field of Search 53/450, 550, 451, 53/551, 468, 563, 570, 469, 386.1, 374.4, 374.5, 373.7, 375.9, 389.3

(56) **References Cited**

U.S. PATENT DOCUMENTS

3,264,794	8/1966	Brown et al. .
3,855,907 *	12/1974	Johnson et al. 53/469
4,021,283 *	5/1977	Weikert 53/469
4,171,605	10/1979	Putnam, Jr. et al. 53/552
4,319,443 *	3/1982	Watts, Jr. 53/466
4,715,166 *	12/1987	Kameda 53/374.4

5,058,364 *	10/1991	Seiden et al. 53/570
5,067,306 *	11/1991	Umezawa 53/551
5,095,960	3/1992	Gründler et al. 141/114
5,255,497 *	10/1993	Zoromski et al. 53/551
5,279,095	1/1994	Müller 53/386.1
5,279,098 *	1/1994	Fukuda 53/551
5,555,709	9/1996	Savigny et al. 53/570
5,590,511 *	1/1997	Morrison 53/374.4
5,715,647 *	2/1998	Keim et al. 53/551
5,755,082 *	5/1998	Takahashi et al. 53/551

FOREIGN PATENT DOCUMENTS

681445 A5	3/1993	(CH) .
1 283 139	11/1968	(DE) .
21 31 126	1/1973	(DE) .
25 20 269	11/1976	(DE) .
28 41 837	5/1979	(DE) .
0 404 719 A1	12/1990	(DE) .
0 685 391 A1	12/1995	(DE) .
RS 97647	11/1996	(EP) .

* cited by examiner

Primary Examiner—Eugene Kim
(74) *Attorney, Agent, or Firm*—Darby & Darby

(57) **ABSTRACT**

A packaging machine is described for forming, filling and sealing bags with a product. The machine forms a film into an elongate, side-sealed tube as it travels in a first direction, and severs the elongate tube into individual, open-ended, bag-length elements. These are then transported in a second direction transverse to the first direction, and a bottom seal formed on them to convert them into open-topped bags. A carousel is arranged to receive the open-topped bags. Product is introduced into each of the open-topped bags, and a top seal formed on each of them to convert them into filled, sealed bags, as the bags travel round the carousel.

27 Claims, 18 Drawing Sheets

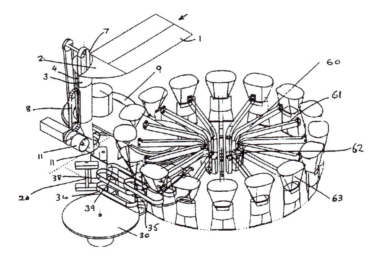

Figure 5.2. Front page, description and claims of an American grant

US 6,199,351 B1

1

PACKAGING MACHINE

BACKGROUND OF THE INVENTION

1. Field of the Invention

This invention relates to a packaging machine and, more particularly, to a machine for packaging snack products (e.g. potato crisps) and other low density materials. A typical use would be to package 30 g portions of crisps in bags 127 mm wide and 178 mm long.

2. Discussion of the Related Art

There is a limit to the speed at which a conventional vertical, form, fill and seal machine can package snacks and other lightweight products. The speed is limited by the maximum rate at which the product can fall and the length of time needed to heat seal the film.

SUMMARY OF THE INVENTION

The present invention uses a method in which the packs preferably travel round on a carousel. Hence much more time is available for the processes involved in forming and filling the bag and the machine operations are less interdependent.

Filling by means of a rotating carousel is already widely used with rigid containers such as in the canning industry, and to a lesser extent with flexible packaging.

Two particular instances of machines which have carousels for the filling of flexible packaging are:

a) A machine produced by Jones & Co. Inc. of Cincinnati, Ohio 45201, USA. In this machine, a reel of flat film is folded longitudinally and then divided into sections by sealing. The pouches so formed have three closed edges and are still joined to one another. The string of pouches passes round a carousel, where product is introduced from a number of chutes. The top seal is then made and the pouches are cut from each other. This type of filling is suited to heavier products such as soups, rice or confectionery, and is in use elsewhere.

b) A machine produced by Thurlings Verpackungsmaschinen GmbH, of D-41749 Viersen, Germany. With this machine, the film is made into bags by conventional vertical, form, fill and seal means (film unwind, tubeformer, vertical seal and jaws). Only one end of each bag is sealed and the open bags already separated from one another, are then transferred to a rotating turret by means of vacuum operating suckers. The turret has a number of stations, each with a number of fingers, which project into each bag and open to hold it in position. The turret indexes round and product is introduced by a chute. After the bag has left the carousel, its top seal is made.

According to a first aspect of the present invention there is provided a packaging machine for forming, filling and sealing bags with a product, which comprises means for forming a film into an elongate, side-sealed tube as it travels in a first direction, means for severing the elongate tube into individual, open-ended, bag-length elements, means for transporting the said elements in a second direction transverse to the first direction, means for forming a bottom seal on said elements to convert them into open-topped bags, a carousel arranged to carry the open-topped bags, and means for introducing product into each of the open-topped bags and for forming a top seal on each of the bags to convert them into filled, sealed bags, as the bags travel round the carousel.

According to another aspect of the invention there is provided a machine for forming a film of heat-sealable film

2

into an elongate, side-sealed tube, comprising a tubeformer for forming the film into shape of a tube with overlapping longitudinal edge portions as it travels from a film supply, inner and outer pressure members which engage the inside and outside of the said edge portions and travel with them, and means for applying heat to the said edge portions.

According to a further aspect of the invention there is provided a device for use in filling open-topped bags with a product, comprising fingers adapted to enter and hold the open top of each bag, and a chute formed of a plurality of members which are movable with respect to one another from a configuration in which the chute can enter the open bag top to an expanded configuration in which product can enter the bag therethrough.

Other aspects of the invention appear from the claims.

BRIEF DESCRIPTION OF THE DRAWING

The invention will now be described with reference to the accompanying drawings, in which:

FIG. 1 shows the general arrangement, in diagrammatic form, of an embodiment of a machine according to the invention;

FIG. 2 shows the complete vertical seal assembly used in the machine of FIG. 1;

FIG. 3 shows a picker for the use in the machine. The embodiment of picker shown in FIG. 3 differs from that shown diagrammatically in FIG. 1;

FIGS. 4a and 4b are a plan view and an elevational view (partly sectional) showing in detail a bottom sealer for use in the machine, the design being similar to the top sealer, the sealer being shown only diagrammatically in FIG. 1;

FIG. 5 shows a cup and finger mechanism, with the cup in its open position;

FIG. 5a shows a detail of FIG. 5, with the cup in its closed position;

FIG. 6 is a perspective view of a modified form of pinch rollers;

FIG. 7 is an exploded perspective view of a preferred design of knife;

FIG. 8 is a perspective view of a modified form of picker mechanism, incorporating transit belts upstream of the picker belts; and

FIGS. 9 to 18 show a modified form of the assembly of cup, fingers and arm carrying the cup and fingers, in which FIG. 9 is a perspective view with the fingers and cup both open, FIG. 10 is a similar view, but with the fingers omitted and the cup closed, FIGS. 11 and 12 are side elevations of the assembly from opposite sides, FIG. 13 is a partly exploded perspective view showing individual components, FIG. 14 is a more completely exploded view, FIG. 15 is a perspective view showing the operation of the fingers, and FIGS. 16 to 18 show the finger mechanism with the fingers respectively open, closing, and closed, some of the components not relevant to the movement of the fingers being omitted from FIGS. 16 to 18.

DESCRIPTION OF THE PREFERRED EMBODIMENTS

The machine shown in FIGS. 1 to 5a of the drawings will firstly be described in more detail, referring to the various sections of which it can be regarded as being composed:

a) Film Handling Mechanisms

The initial film handling mechanisms use techniques already employed with existing vertical, form, fill and seal

Figure 5.2. (contd.)

US 6,199,351 B1

7

generally vertical axis. A lug 133 extends from the radially outer edge of the load cam 132 and is positioned to be engaged by one arm of an L-shaped trigger 134 which is pivotally connected to the block 126 for movement about a generally horizontal axis. FIG. 15 also shows a striker post 135 which is fixedly mounted on the frame of the carousel (i.e. it does not rotate with the carousel) and which is arranged so that in one position of the arm in its rotation with the carousel, for which see below, the lower arm of the L-shaped trigger 134 strikes it.

The upper ends of the pins 128 are held in a slot 136 formed in the underside of a plunger 137 which is spring biased in a radially outward direction by a compression spring 138 whose other end bears against the cross-member 106 (see, for example, FIG. 9). It should be noted that when the cup is open the distance between the cross-member 106 and the plunger 137 is much greater than when the cup is closed. The size of the spring, and its spring constant are chosen so that in the former condition it exerts very little force on the plunger, whereas in the latter condition it exerts a substantial force. This means that when the cup is open the fingers are urged apart only lightly and are not able to open the bag sideways and thus flatten it. This is clearly advantageous, in that the object of the open cup is to enable product to be introduced into the bag. A resetting rod 139 is connected at its radially outer end by a ball joint to the load cam 132 and is slidably guided adjacent its other end by a guide member 140 connected to the arm 100 for pivotal movement about a horizontal axis with respect thereto. The radially inner end 141 of the resetting rod is arranged to bear over a given segment of the rotation of the assembly against a cam disc 142 (see FIG. 17).

A description will now be given of the operation of the assembly of FIGS. 9 to 18, in relation to its rotation with the carousel through 360°. The sequence of events which takes place is as follows (it must be understood that the angles are approximate, and can vary substantially from machine to machine):

0°: The arm 101, which is at an intermediate height, starts to drop into the bag which is being held open by the vacuum belts, the fingers being closed as shown in FIG. 18. Lowering of the arm is under the control of engagement between the cam 103 and the cam follower 102. The cup is in a closed condition.

5°: Continued lowering of the arm causes the trigger 134 to strike the post 135 (see FIG. 15, where contact has just been made), which then causes the trigger to rotate. This in turn produces rotation of the load cam 132, via its lug 133. The load cam is no longer in a position to keep the cam followers 129 apart, and the crank arms 127 therefore rotate under the force applied to their pins 128 by the spring 138, so moving the fingers 125 to their open position (FIG. 16). Shortly after this position the arm becomes fully lowered (horizontal).

10°: The cup-controlling cam follower 120 engages the cam 121 (FIG. 10) and starts to move the outer cup half 115 radially outwardly. By virtue of the double-armed lever 104, the inner cup half 109 simultaneously starts to move radially inwardly. Thus, the cup begins to open.

20°: The cup is now fully open (FIG. 9).

45°–90°: Product is introduced into the bag through the open cup as the arm rotates through this range.

180°: The radius of the cam 121 begins to reduce, causing the outer cup half 115 to begin to move radially inwards, and, by virtue of the double armed lever 104,

8

causing the inner cup half 109 simultaneously to begin to move radially outwards. Thus, the cup begins to close.

200°: The cup is fully closed and the bag is held by the fingers. The arm starts to lift as a result of re-engagement of the cam follower 102 with the cam 103.

230°: The arm reaches an intermediate height, ready to transfer the bags to the top seal belts.

250°: The fingers are reset to their closed position by engagement of the resetting rod 139 with the cam disc 142 (FIG. 17).

270°: The arm reaches its maximum height to clear the top seal mechanism.

315°: The arm starts to drop down.

360°: As 0°.

What is claimed is:

1. A packaging machine for continuous operation for forming, filling and sealing bags of a product comprising: means for forming a film into an elongate, side-sealed tube as it travels in a first direction, means for severing the elongate tube into individual, open-ended, bag-length elements, belt means for transporting the said elements in a second direction transverse to the first direction, means for forming a bottom seal on said elements to convert them into open-topped bags, a carousel in-line with said transporting means that are continuously moving for receiving the open-topped bags as the open-topped bags travel tangentially to said carousel at a speed substantially matching that of said carousel, so that the transport means transport said elements continuously onto said continuously moving carousel, and means for introducing product into each of the open-topped bags and for forming a top seal on each of the bags to convert them into filled, sealed bags, as the bags are moved round the carousel.

2. A machine according to claim 1, wherein said film is a heat-sealable film and wherein the means for forming the film into an elongate, side-sealed tube, comprises a tube-former for forming the film into the shape of a tube with overlapping longitudinal edge portions as it travels from a film supply, inner and outer pressure members which engage the inside and outside of the said edge portions and travel with them, and means for supplying heat to the said edge portions.

3. A machine according to claim 2, wherein the inner and outer pressure members are belts.

4. A machine according to claim 1, further comprising a pair of pinch rollers for engaging opposite faces of the side-sealed tube, at least one of the rollers having a pair of lands extending radially therefrom and arranged to engage the tube on either side of the side seal, the side seal itself being arranged to pass between the pinch rollers without pressure being exerted thereon.

5. A machine claim 1, wherein the said severing means comprises a pair of rotatable rollers disposed with their axes of rotation parallel to one another and offset by an acute angle from a direction at right angles to the direction of film travel, one of the rollers having an anvil surface, and the other of the rollers having an elongate cutting member adapted to cuttingly engage the said anvil surface, the cutting member running at a right angle to the direction of film travel.

6. A machine claim 1, wherein the means for transporting them in said second direction comprises a picker mechanism having means for receiving open-ended bag-length elements travelling in said first direction and means for gripping the said elements and causing them to move in said second direction.

Figure 5.2. (contd.)

The national classification numbers for this patent are given at code (52). This is taken from the highly detailed scheme which emphasises applications, or products, rather than ideas. The IPC numbers on the patents are derived from a computer concordance to the American classification, and are often regarded as being somewhat unreliable. They frequently refer to a single, broader topic rather than to two or more more detailed concepts.

The "references cited" at code (56) constitute the search report. This information has been given in American patents and designs since 1947. It is always arranged in order so that American patents are given first, then foreign patents, then "other publications", which are usually books, journal articles, conferences or catalogues. Chemical and electronics patents in particular often have many journal or conference citations. Against each American patent is given the month and year of publication, the inventor and the US classification number which has caused the examiner to cite the patent on the grounds of relevance. The inventors' names are omitted for the foreign patent documents. Sometimes the search report goes over onto the following page. Since January 2001 an asterisk has been added to any citations which were cited by the examiner alone rather than by the applicant in the initial "invention disclosure".

Although unlike many other countries' search reports the degree of relevance to the specification in question is not stated, this is less serious than it may seem as the patent has already been granted, and the report does not assist the searcher wondering if an application is likely to be granted. The fact that every patent will have some sort of search report — even if it cites catalogues of goods — makes the American search reports of great potential use. It is easy to go back in time using these search reports but from 1976 it is also possible to go forward in time to find later patents that referred back to a known patent. This is possible on the official Patent Full Text and Image Database at **http://www.uspto.gov/patft/index.html** by using the "Referenced by" link on the text (not image) part of each record.

Those grants that were formerly published as PCT applications will have the PCT number and date of publication at code (87).

The front page is followed by drawings. The remainder of the specification is often very structured, although the exact wording may vary, and sometimes the order. The following is typical, with each heading prominently centred and in capitals: Related application(s); Background of the invention; Summary of the invention; Brief description of the drawings; Detailed description (or, Description of preferred embodiments). The numbered claims then follow, introduced simply as "What is claimed is".

The background section usually gives a large amount of detail about prior art, with references to patents or journal articles. The description is also detailed, often with more information than foreign patents would give. Applications abroad by foreign companies that bear the headings given above can be taken as an implication that there is, or will be, a corresponding American patent, and are likely to include the same amount of detail.

Copies of American specifications are available as Adobe Acrobat copies on **Esp@cenet** at **http://gb.espacenet.com** back to 1920 and on the official Patent Full-Text and Full-Image Databases site at **http://www.uspto.gov/patft/index.html** back to 1836 (but a choice of other software must be installed). These include the other varieties of patent documents. There are also CD-ROM products.

The gazette

The *Official Gazette* is published weekly. The patents in each issue are divided into three sections: General and Mechanical, Chemical and Electrical. Within each section they are arranged in US classification order. Since the classification does not neatly divide into the three subject areas it means that there are effectively three classified sequences in each issue.

The patents are numbered after they have been classified and arranged within these sections so that they form a single numerical sequence. Bibliographic details are given for each patent. This includes references to related applications, priority data and to the PCT and can be quite complex. A representative illustration and usually a single claim, which in effect forms an abstract, is given. This is usually the first claim but sometimes a later claim is considered to be more useful in indicating the inventive step.

Each issue has a single index of the patentees and assignees, and another arranged by US classification.

These indexes have references from the assignees to the patentees, where the title information is given. The entry for the patentees give the name of any assignee. Similar indexes for each calendar year are also published.

Nowadays it is more normal to search online and to rely on the most recent specifications appearing at the top of the page for current awareness.

Abstracts

The USA does not publish separate abstracts of its patents (although they are provided on the front pages). Bibliographic details and the first, or what is considered to be the main, claim, together with a drawing, are published in numerical order in its gazette.

Derwent Publications publishes *USA Patents Abstracts* weekly in three sections: Chemical; Mechanical and general; and Electrical. They provide bibliographic details, an abstract and if relevant a drawing for each patent. The abstracts are published in Derwent's own classified order but with a numerical concordance.

There are CD-ROM products which index and provide abstracts of American patents. Examples are MicroPatent's US PatentSearch, which provides abstracts and many searching fields back to 1969 on several discs, and CASSIS, which provides less information on a single Bibliographic disc back to 1969 and on a Class disc. The Class disc provides classified lists of all patents back to 1836 and the current classification of a particular patent.

Abstracts on the Internet are available as shown at the end of the "Specifications" section back to 1976.

Other forms of patent documents

American patents are officially called utility patents to distinguish them from design patents, which are for the appearance of an object.

All American forms of patent documents since 2 January 2001 have codes following the number. These forms, and the codes that they may bear as a suffix, are:

Design patents (coded S, but better known as being prefixed by D)
Plant patents (P2, but better known as being prefixed by PP. Codes P2, P3, P4 and P9 may also be used).
Reissues (E, but better known as being prefixed by RE)
Statutory inventions (H)

Design patents began in 1842 but did not include a drawing until 1892. They are numbered from no. 1 in 1842 with the first in 2001 being D435,713.

The USA is the only country to allow **plant patents** for new plant varieties. They are numbered in a series from no. 1 in 1931 with the first in 2001 being PP 11,728.

If a published American patent is found to be inaccurate, due to, for instance, printing errors, then the patent and its number is replaced by a **Reissue** (Re) specification. They are numbered in a series from no. 1 in 1838 with the first in 2001 being Re 37,006.

If, on the other hand, through opposition in the courts the patent is amended then a **Reexamination** certificate is published. They keep the patent number and were formerly coded as B documents, commonly B1 (the number indicates the number of times a B is issued for the patent). Both the certificate and an entry in the gazette indicate what has been altered. From 2 January 2001 they are coded as C1 etc. (again the number indicates the number of times a C is issued for the patent).

Deliberate disclosures are possible where the applicant describes the invention in such detail that nobody can take out a patent. These have bibliographical details and are printed in full. No other country has such a system. These disclosures were formerly called **Defensives** (coded T), and from 1984 were called **Statutory Inventions**. Their designation is H with the first in 2001 being H 1930.

Claims and bibliographic details for all these categories are published in the gazette.

Patent Cooperation Treaty applications designating the USA

Granted patents have at INID code (87) the PCT number and date of publication. Prior to the publication of applications from March 2001 no translations of PCTs in foreign languages were published in the American systems nor was there any data on entry or non-entry in the national phase.

Those applications filed in the PCT system which designate the United States will be published as applications under the new system in their entirety, either in the original English or in translation.

Case law

The American procedure in patent litigation is different from that in Britain. There are no specialised courts or judges and juries are used. However, since 1982 there has been the Court of Appeals on the Federal Circuit which (among other specialised areas) hears appeals in patent cases. A reason to set it up was to relieve the burden on the regional courts of appeal and on the Supreme Court. The main journal of record is *United States Patents Quarterly* (often called USPQ). Sites on patent cases, including those of the US Patent Office's own courts (for refused applications) are listed under the USA in our list of patent litigation sites at **http://www.bl.uk/services/information/patents/ othlink3.html#lit**.

The British Library and United States patents

A microfiche concordance is available at the British Library for filing numbers from 1968, although it is not up to date, and more recent publications can be traced on CD-ROM, using the US PatentSearch discs, or the SNAP concordance discs. Nowadays such work is mostly done on the web.

If a Reissue is published then the British Library places a reference at the original document. For minor printing errors or for reexamination B1, B2 etc. certificates this is attached to the original. These only apply to the paper series which ceased with the beginning of the year 2000.

Patent applications from US government agencies (but lacking the claims and the front page information) were formerly received at the British Library and reduced the delay in seeing the information. They are entitled "US government owned applications" at the British Library and are numbered by the application number preceded by a number indicating the sequence of filing numbers running from 1 to 1 million. A recent number in this series, for example, is 8-553161. This series seems to have been discontinued.

Internet databases

These are extremely numerous and this can only be a summary. Probably the most useful free sources are the official Patent Full-Text and Full-Page Image Databases at **http://www.uspto.gov/patft/index.html**. It contains images from 1836 and searchable text (including the entire specification) from 1976. Newly published applications and grants appear on day of publication (Thursdays and Tuesdays respectively). By using US classification the patents to 1836 can be searched. The images run on software downloaded from the site. The DEPATISnet site offers Adobe Acrobat copies back to 1836 at **http://www.depatisnet.de**.

The **Esp@cenet** site at **http://gb.espacenet.com** is very popular and has Adobe Acrobat copies back to 1836.

Those files for the USA known are listed under US at the British Library site **http://www.bl.uk/services/information/patents/othlink2.html#singe**.

Derwent Information in their English abstracts used their own codes DT for the OS and DS for either the AS or the PS stage and these may appear in references. DT was in fact the old country code for (West) Germany.

With 1981 legislation the AS stage was dropped and only the OS and PS stages became possible. These are coded as A1 and C2 if both are published, but about 15% of the time only the PS is published, as a C1.

These stages and codes can be summarised as follows.

Stage	Common German code	Document code	Derwent code
Offenlegungsschrift	OS	A1	DT
Auslegeschrift	AS	B2	DS
Patentschrift	PS	C1 or C2	DS

European and PCT applications have been treated in a special way. From 1983 translations of the claims of European applications in English or French that designated Germany were published with the European number followed by T1. Within the annual numeration there were special sequences beginning with 60001 and 90001 for European patents and PCTs (national phase) respectively. The latter could be republished as C2s if granted. The Inpadoc database coded the 60001 range informally as CO and the 90001 range as T documents. The 60001 range was replaced from 1989 as explained below.

The most recent change (from 1995) is that the whole system of numeration altered and included utility models (a lesser form of protection), trade marks and designs. The first digit of the number indicates the type of document; the next two digits signify the last two digits of the year; the following digits indicate the number given to the application within that year. The numbers are assigned to each filing number when applied for in Germany itself (and hence also to the publication).

These first digits are as follows:

1 = patent
2 = utility model
3 = trade marks
4 = designs
5 = European grants designating Germany, which were in German
6 = European grants designating Germany, which were in English or French

A quick way to distinguish them from earlier numbers is that the older numbers had seven digits but these new numbers have eight digits. Only some Japanese and American numbers are likely to have so many digits.

Within both the 1 and 2 series there are allocated number ranges. These are:

1 series (patents)

00001 – 74999 = patent application
75000 – 79999 = supplementary protection certificates (SPCs) for pharmaceuticals
80000 – 99999 = PCT application

2 series (utility models)
00001 – 74999 = utility model application
75000 – 79999 = semiconductor topographies
80000 – 99999 = PCT application

The 5 and 6 series were used for filings at the European Patent Office made from 1 December 1989. For patents and utility models, the change occurred with filings made in 1995. Hence 19520000 was no. 20,000 filed in 1995 among the patents.

The 6 series will contain a translation (*übersetzung*) of the European grant from the English or French and is coded T2. The European number is given above a number like 697 02 200 at code (97). They may be referred to as CO specifications.

Outside of these numerical series is a series of translations of the claims of European patent applications that designated Germany and which were in English or French. These are published in the format DE/EP 0 797 637 where 797 637 is the European number. They are coded T1.

The utility models, or *Gebrauchsmuster*, often called GM, are for simpler inventions (mainly mechanical or electrical) and began in 1891. They were numbered in a continuous sequence up until 1968 to 1,990,000 and then within the year of application from 66000001 (that is, 1966) onwards. German speakers when speaking in English refer to these specifications as "designs" but the German word for what we would call a design is *Geschmacksmuster*. As indicated earlier from 1995 their numbers were changed, so that a typical number is 29920000 for a filing made in 1999. They have never had filing numbers and were numbered when applied for. They are coded as U1 documents but were coded as U before the 1995 change to the series beginning with 2.

Patenting procedure

To a large extent this section summarises what has just been explained in the last section.

The grants were published from the beginning of the system in 1877 as *Patentschriften* or PS documents. From 1957 an earlier stage, the *Auslegeschrift* or AS was published. From 1968 an earlier still stage, the *Offenlegungsschrift* or OS was published. In 1981 the AS stage was abolished. These codes are frequently used to indicate the different kinds of publication.

Normally the two stages, OS and PS, are published. However the OS stage can be omitted. This is because the applicant has up to seven years from the filing of the OS document to decide whether or not to ask for an examination. By quickly asking for examination, about 15% of the PS specifications are published 18 months from the priority date. The publication stages are coded (since 1968) as A (OS), B (for the old AS) and C (PS) followed by a number indicating the number of times that it has been published in the system. A1 is common and C2 means a PS published after an earlier OS, while a C1 indicates that it was published only as a PS.

The PS is open to opposition for 3 months from the date of publication so that others can dispute its validity. The patent runs for 20 years from the date of filing provided that renewal fees are paid. Extra terms are possible for pharmaceuticals to allow for loss of protection due to awaiting permission to market the drug and *Schutzzertifikate* denote the certificates allowing extra time.

The utility models or *Gebrauchsmuster*, often called GM, are simpler inventions. Until 1990 they only covered non-chemical fields and they still cannot be used for processes. They are not examined, and are normally published a few months after filing (but some may be delayed for years). Protection is given for a maximum of 10 years. It is possible to switch a patent application to a utility model if the new aspects are considered too obvious to be allowed as a patent.

The merger of the Federal Republic of Germany with the German Democratic Republic on 3 October 1990 did not initially mean any changes to the documentation. This was because the pending East German applications at the time of the merger continued to be published as DD patents, or to be abstracted in the old East German gazette, the *Bekanntmachungen*. Applicants were given the option to continue a pending application through the West German system. Applications after 3 October 1990 had to go through the Munich office as (West) German applications, and the old East German material will eventually cease to be published as DD patents once they have all been dealt with. The last issue of the *Bekanntmachungen* was published on 25 June 1992. From then on relevant material was published as Teil 8 in the *Patentblatt*.

Legislation in the summer of 1991 means that the old East and West German patents have protection retrospectively extended to all of Germany. It had been provisionally decided to allow them protection only in the old jurisdictions.

Specifications

Some key terms that might be found in German patent specifications or the DEPATISnet database are as follows:

Ansprüch = claim★
Auszüge = abstracts
Beispiel = example
Beschreibung = description★
Erfinder = inventor
Erfindung = invention
Erteilung = grant
Patentinhaber = applicant
Prüfungsantrag = request for examination
Seite = page
Vertreter = patent agent
Zeichnung = drawing
Zusammenfassung = abstract

★ The German words may be preceded by "Patent".

The front page of a typical *Offenlegungsschrift* or OS is shown in Figure 6.1. It was filed on 22 December 2000 (code (22), Anmeldetag) when it was given the number 100 64 786 A 1. It was published (code (43), Offenlegungstag) on 28 June 2001. Code (30) gives the

American priority details. No search report is normally published at this stage (but some will have one). The following pages of an OS would have the description, claims and then any drawings.

The front page of a typical *Patentschrift* or PS is shown in Figure 6.2. It was numbered 198 18 503 C2 because it was filed in 1998 and was a C2 because it was published initially as an A1 with the same number (the date of which is given at code (43)). The date of its grant, 24 February 2000, is given at code (45). A C1 specification would lack a code (43).

The search report is given at code (56). It consists of a German OS, DE 43 40 573 A1; four German utility models, all coded U1; and one French and one British specification. The usage of codes is inconsistent and sometimes terms like OS and GM are used.

The front page of a typical utility model is shown in Figure 6.3. It is numbered 201 01 000 U 1 and is only published in the one stage. It was registered (granted) without any substantive examination for novelty on 29 March 2001 as shown by code (47) and this was announced in the *Patentblatt* on 3 May 2001 as shown by code (43). The inventor is not named and only the applicant at code (73). During 2000 they began to have abstracts and drawings on the front page as shown here. The remainder of the specification was similar to a patent.

All German patent and utility model documents are available on CD-ROMs from 1991. In addition, copies of the patent specifications may be available on the Internet.

The **Esp@cenet** database at **http://gb.espacenet.com** provides Adobe Acrobat copies of German specifications from 1877 if the patent number is known. This may be the OS rather than the PS. German utility models are available for publications from 1985 (they can be selected by using DEU in the publication number field). The DEPATISnet database at **http://www.depatisnet.de** appears to have Adobe Acrobat copies of all German patents plus that of some utility models. The entire description and claims can be searched (in German) from 1987 onwards.

The gazette

The *Patentblatt* has been Germany's patent gazette since 1877 and is published weekly. It lacks any abstracts or illustations. The cover lists the different categories (Teils) with the relevant pagination. The main Teils are 1 for published applications, 3 for grants, 4 for utility models, 5 for European grants and 6 for the Patent Cooperation Treaty. Generally a classified sequence is found in section (a) of each Teil. Teil 9 is for former East German material. A single name index to Teils 1 to 6 is on yellow pages at the back of each issue.

Abstracts

There are a number of gazettes, all of which are published weekly. They give claims rather than abstracts plus if relevant a drawing.

The *Patentblatt* lists in IPC order bibliographic details of published patents. Cumulated indexes of applicants are published twice a year. The *Auszüge aus den Offenlegungschriften* is

⑩ **BUNDESREPUBLIK DEUTSCHLAND**

DEUTSCHES PATENT- UND MARKENAMT

⑫ **Offenlegungsschrift**

⑩ **DE 100 64 786 A 1**

㉑ Aktenzeichen: 100 64 786.3
㉒ Anmeldetag: 22. 12. 2000
㊸ Offenlegungstag: 28. 6. 2001

㉕ Int. Cl.⁷:
H 01 J 35/12

DE 100 64 786 A 1

㉚ Unionspriorität:
472549　　27. 12. 1999　US

㉛ Anmelder:
General Electric Co., Schenectady, N.Y., US

㉔ Vertreter:
Tiedtke, Bühling, Kinne & Partner, 80336 München

㉒ Erfinder:
Snyder, Douglas J., Brookfield, Wis., US

Die folgenden Angaben sind den vom Anmelder eingereichten Unterlagen entnommen

㉔ Röntgenröhren-Dampfkammertarget

㉗ Die Erfindung bezieht sich auf eine Röntgenröhre zum Emittieren von Röntgenstrahlen, die ein Gehäuse (22), einen Anodenaufbau, der im Gehäuse (22) angeordnet ist und eine Targetfläche umfasst, einen Kathodenaufbau, der in das Gehäuse (22) mit einem Abstand vom Anodenaufbau eingebaut ist, und einen Targetkörper aufweist, der sich von der Targetfläche des Anodenaufbaus aus erstreckt. Der Kathodenaufbau umfasst eine Elektronen emittierende Elektronenemissionseinrichtung. Die Elektronen treffen auf die Targetfläche des Anodenaufbaus und erzeugen Röntgenstrahlen. Der Targetkörper weist einen Hohlraum auf, der ein Arbeitsfluid enthält und dazu ausgelegt ist, thermische Energie von der Targetfläche wegzutransportieren.

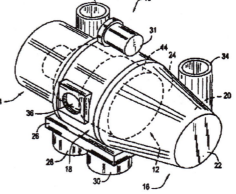

DE 100 64 786 A 1

BUNDESDRUCKEREI　05.01　102 026/217/1　　13

Figure 6.1. Front page of a German application

(19) **BUNDESREPUBLIK DEUTSCHLAND**

DEUTSCHES PATENT- UND MARKENAMT

(12) **Patentschrift**

(10) **DE 198 18 503 C 2**

(51) Int. Cl.⁷:
B 60 N 3/00
B 60 R 7/04
B 60 R 7/08
B 60 N 2/44
A 45 F 4/06
A 47 G 9/06

(21) Aktenzeichen: 198 18 503.0-21
(22) Anmeldetag: 24. 4. 1998
(43) Offenlegungstag: 4. 11. 1999
(45) Veröffentlichungstag der Patenterteilung: 24. 2. 2000

DE 198 18 503 C 2

Innerhalb von 3 Monaten nach Veröffentlichung der Erteilung kann Einspruch erhoben werden

(73) Patentinhaber:
Schaaf, Christian, 84028 Landshut, DE; Goller, Joerg, 84184 Tiefenbach, DE

(74) Vertreter:
Meissner, Bolte & Partner, 80538 München

(72) Erfinder:
gleich Patentinhaber

(56) Für die Beurteilung der Patentfähigkeit in Betracht gezogene Druckschriften:

DE	43 40 573 A1
DE	2 97 17 960 U1
DE	2 95 16 115 U1
DE	2 96 14 368 U1
DE	92 06 820 U1
FR	27 37 447 A1
GB	22 78 271 A

(54) **Multifunktionales Gestell**

(57) Multifunktionales Gestell, insbesondere zum Befestigen an der Rückenlehne eines Fahrzeugsitzes, mit
– einer ersten und einer zweiten, über ein Gelenk verbundenen Fläche (7, 8), wobei die Flächen (7, 8) zum Gelenk hin im wesentlichen symmetrisch ausgebildet sind,
– einer am Gelenk angeschlagenen winkelverstellbaren dritten Fläche (9) mit seitlich angeordneten Abspannmitteln (10) zum Erhalt einer vorgegebenen Lage bezogen auf die erste und/oder zweite Fläche (7, 8),
– mindestens einen an der ersten und/oder der zweiten Fläche (8) befestigbaren Montagegurt (11), und mit
– einer elastischen Rahmung (1, 2, 3), durch die die Flächen (7, 8, 9) formstabil gehalten sind, wobei die Flächen (7, 8, 9) aus einem textilen oder Ledermaterial bestehen.

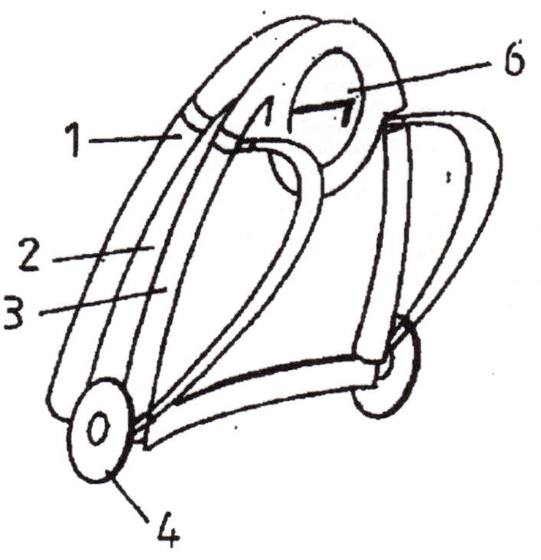

DE 198 18 503 C 2

BUNDESDRUCKEREI 12.99 902 168/213/9 15

Figure 6.2. Front page of a German grant

(19) **BUNDESREPUBLIK DEUTSCHLAND**

(12) **Gebrauchsmusterschrift**

(10) **DE 201 01 000 U 1**

(51) Int. Cl.⁷:
E 05 D 5/02

DEUTSCHES PATENT- UND MARKENAMT

(21) Aktenzeichen: 201 01 000.3
(22) Anmeldetag: 12. 1. 2001
(47) Eintragungstag: 29. 3. 2001
(43) Bekanntmachung im Patentblatt: 3. 5. 2001

DE 201 01 000 U 1

(73) Inhaber:
Topic GmbH, Sarleinsbach, AT

(74) Vertreter:
P. Meissner und Kollegen, 14199 Berlin

(54) An einer Zarge, einem Stock o.dgl., befestigbarer Beschlag

(57) An einer eine Türöffnung (1) begrenzenden Zarge (3), einem Stock od. dgl., befestigbarer Beschlag, in dem mindestens eine durch wenigstens eine Öffnung (10) zugängliche Aufnahme für einen diese Öffnung(en) (10) in seiner Schließstellung durchsetzende(n) Schlossriegel eines in einem Türblatt (4) angeordneten Schlosses vorgesehen ist, dadurch gekennzeichnet, dass ein an einer zur Türblattebene parallelen Außenfläche (5) der Zarge (3), des Stockes od. dgl., befestigbares, massives Metallgehäuse (6) vorgesehen ist, das mit einem abstehenden, an einer zur Türblattebene senkrechten Außenfläche (7) der Zarge (3), des Stockes od. dgl., anliegenden Flansch (8) versehen ist.

DE 201 01 000 U 1

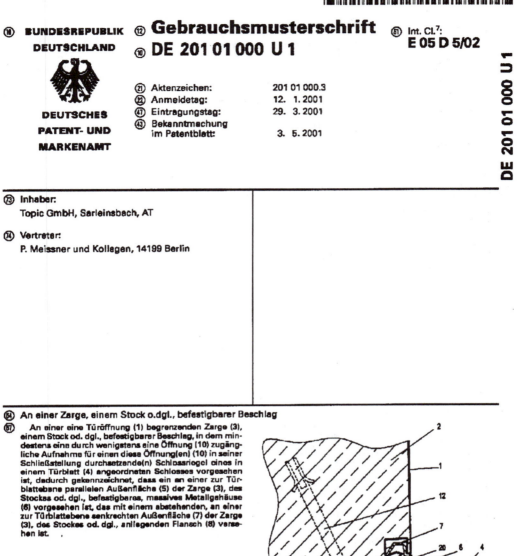

BUNDESDRUCKEREI 03.01 102 218/234/30A 1

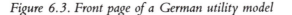

Figure 6.3. Front page of a German utility model

divided into three series, Teil 1 to 3, according to the subject matter. They consist of classified arrangements of the main claims, with a drawing, of the *Offenlegungsschrift* documents.

The *Auszüge aus den Patentschriften* is a similar publication. Since many documents are published for the first time as *Patentschriften* it is a useful series for alerting purposes.

The utility models have a similar publication, the *Auszüge aus den Gebrauchsmustern*.

Derwent Information publishes the *German Patents Abstracts* (previously *German Patents Gazette*), in three subject series, which cover the *Offenlegungsschriften*, and the German Patents Abstracts, examined series, in two subject series, for the Patentschriften.

The DEPATISnet database at **http://www.depatisnet.de** has (German language) abstracts from 1981. The **Esp@cenet** database at **http://gb.espacenet.com** has English abstracts on its "worldwide" option to about the mid 1980s.

The DEPAROM CD-ROMs contain bibliographic details and the main claim of German OS and PS specifications from 1980, and of utility models from 1983.

Patent Cooperation Treaty applications designating Germany

Formerly in the old German numeration where the initial digits were 18 plus 50 to make the year of filing PCT applications were given their own number range. This was 90001 onwards. From 1995 PCT applications designating Germany were numbered in special number ranges within the annual sequences in the 1 (patents) and 2 (utility model) sequences. In both cases this was an 80000 to 99999 range.

Case law

The journal *Blatt für Patent-, Muster- und Zeichenblatt* has been published since 1948. Among other things it includes court cases.

The *Entscheidungen des Bundespatentgerichts* has been published annually since 1962. It gives legal decisions by the Federal German Patent Court and is arranged by subject.

Three websites give a great deal of free information: BGH-free at **http://www.rws-verlag.de/bgh-free/indexfre.htm**, Bundesverfassungsgericht at **http://www.bundesverfassungsgericht.de/cgi-bin/link.pl?entscheidungen** and GLAW: German case law at **http://www.uni-wuerzburg.de/glaw/index.html**.

The British Library and the German patents

The British Library keeps the three types of German specifications (OS, AS and PS) in separate sequences, but since a patent application always retains its original number it is easy to check for the most recent publication. In addition there are registers indicating what stage an application has reached. The Library ceased receiving German patent specifications on paper in April 2002.

None of the documents in the two supplementary number ranges for EPO or PCT specifications, or for supplementary protection certificates or topographies, are held at the British Library other than any on the CD-ROMs held. Utility models are only held on CD-ROM (from 1991). Before then there are only brief details including a claim and a drawing in the *Auszüge aus den Gebrauchsmustern*.

Internet databases

The DEPATISnet database at **http://www.depatisnet.de** has (German language) abstracts from 1981 and has images of, apparently, all patents plus some utility models. It has an English language interface. The **Esp@cenet** database at **http://gb.espacenet.com** has all patents plus utility models from about 1990.

The official site DPMApatentblatt at **http://www.patentblatt.de** is free (but requires registration) and provides data and images of the last two years' patents and utility models. It has an English language interface.

Contact information

Deutsches Patentamt
D-80297
Munich
Germany

Tel: +49 (0) 89 21950
Fax: +49 (0) 89 21952221

Email: info@dpma.de
Web address: **http://www.dpma.de**

Further reading

German Patent Bulletin in assistant mode on the WWW: the first year's experience. M. Knobel, *World Patent Information*, 2001, 23 (1), 79-81.

The enforcement of patent rights in Germany. H. Marshall, *IIC*, 2000, 31 (6), 646-668.

The unification of Germany and its effect on patents, T. Reimann and J. Feldges, *Patent World*, Dec 1990/Jan 1991, 28, 31-35.

7.   THE JAPANESE PATENT SYSTEM

Japanese patents have a formidable reputation because of the language barrier for most Westerners. A less obvious problem is that of numeration. This chapter is written for the Westerner with little or no understanding of Japanese.

In 1999 there were 405,655 applications filed for patents of which 45,475 (11.2%) were by foreigners. 150,059 patents were registered (granted) in that year of which 16,099 (10.7%) were by foreigners. These compare with 1990 when there were 367,590 filings and 59,401 were registered. There are also utility models, which provide a lesser level of protection. In 1999 9,959 were registered while in 1990 43,300 had been registered.

Japanese A specifications are numbered within each year while the first B specification to be numbered in 2001 was JP 3121501 B2.

Numeration and document codes

Special care should be taken with Japanese patent numeration as it is complicated, and until recently could in theory refer to six different series. It usually consists of three (sometimes four) elements: (sometimes a prefix for the reign), a prefix for the year, a number and a document code. Any known citations should always be copied as given and any extra information (such as subject or applicant) should always be noted. The source of the data should be noted in case of queries.

The first element is the name given to the Emperor's reign. The Emperor Hirohito ruled from 1925 to January 1989 and his reign was called *Showa*, usually shortened to S. In January 1989 the Emperor Akihito came to the throne and his reign is called *Heisei*, usually shortened to H. This element is often not given in citations.

The second element is an indication of the year. Until 1996 (for second stage examined specifications) or 2000 (for published applications) this was a number which indicated the number of years since the beginning of the Emperor's reign. Filing numbers still use this system. Hence a number in the first weeks of 1989 (just before the Emperor Hirohito's death) was prefixed by 64 as that was the 64th year of his reign. The remainder of 1989 was Year 1 of the Emperor Akihito's reign, a numeration which continued to be used until largely superseded after the end of 1999 (in which year it had reached Year 11). In 1996 the third stage grants began to be numbered in a continuous series beginning with 2,500,001, while from 2000 the published applications began to use Western years in annual sequences, hence 2000, 2001 and so on.

The third element is the actual number assigned to the specification. This was a number which began for each series of numbers with 1 in the year (either Imperial or Western) in question and which began a fresh sequence the following year.

The final element is a document code. The published applications are coded A while the published grants are coded B2. This element is sometimes omitted.

The differences with utility models are explained further on in this section.

Chemical Abstracts cites Japanese published applications as e.g. "Jpn. Kokai Tokkyo Koho JP 2001 122,639" which helps to identify it as an A specification (although cited in the printed number index as an A2). *Kokai* means "unexamined" and is frequently used as shorthand to mean a Japanese A specification. *Tokkyo Koho* means "patent gazette".

The second stage of publication used to be the middle stage, and was called *kokoku* ("examined"). These specifications were coded B2. The final stage was of *toroku* ("registered") specifications which were numbered in a continuous series. From 29 May 1996 the final stage was abolished (although used for earlier applications) and was incorporated in the previously middle, second stage which began to be numbered from 2,500,001 onwards and are now called *toroku*. They are normally coded B2 but some are published for the first time (omitting the *kokai* stage) when they are coded as B1 specifications.

The chart below explains how numbers can expect to be seen.

Year first affected	Filing numbers	Published A	Published B	Third, registered
1989	64-1 etc. or 1-1 etc.	64-1 etc. or 1-1 etc.	64-1 etc. or 1-1 etc.	1,471,001 etc.
1996	7-1 etc.	7-1 etc.	2,500,001 etc.	(abolished)
2000	12-1 etc.	2001-1 etc.	2,996,501 etc.	

Utility models were formerly numbered in an identical format to the patents, with abbreviated versions of the specifications as the first, U documents and Y specifications as the second stage. They too had a registered stage numbered in a sequence which reached 1,738,000 in 1989. The U specifications were called *Jitsuyo Shinan Koho*.

From 26 July 1994 the old Y stage and the registered stage were abolished (although earlier filings continue to appear as Ys). There is now only the full specification, with the code U, which is numbered in a 3,000,001 onwards continuous series. From 5 June 1996 the remaining Ys were numbered in a 2,500,001 onwards series. Formerly utility models were popular, but law changes have meant that less than 10,000 are now published annually.

Numbers within the 500,001 onwards range of the published unexamined *kokai* applications within each year are used for translations of Patent Cooperation Treaty applications that designate Japan. Numbers within the 700,001 onwards range of the published unexamined *kokai* applications within each year are used for Supplementary Protection Certificates for extensions of terms for pharmaceutical patents.

Inpadoc data cites B2 documents as B4 documents. Derwent Information's databases and publications used the last two digits of the Western year instead of the Japanese year to indicate the old examined, B2 series. Hence for example 97 was used for Imperial year 9 (1997).

If a B2 is reissued with amendments it is coded H. If a U is reissued with amendments it is coded I.

Newly published Japanese numbers are getting much easier to understand. Formerly a number like 5-20000 could be any of six sequences (patent filing, utility model filing, A, B, U or Y). Now 12-20000 can only be either a patent filing or a utility model filing.

Most requests are for the A, *kokai* specifications. The utility models are rarely requested. The old granted series are in between along with the B specifications.

Unexamined applications have only been published since 1970 so 44 or lower *Showa* years can only be the examined stage (if not a filing number).

Examined documents before 1996 never numbered above 89,000, so higher numbers will clearly be for filings or unexamined applications.

If uncertain then the citation can be looked up on the web to see if the IPC number or abstract sounds correct. The drawings in the *kokai* and examined documents can also be compared to see which appears to be on the right technology.

Patenting procedure

In a sense this restates what has already had to be given in the previous sections.

Japan publishes the unexamined patent application, or *kokai*, 18 months after the priority date. The letter A is prominently given at the top right of the front page. Applications filed before 1971 were only published once.

Until 2001 the applicant had seven years from the date of filing before examination had to be asked for. This will change to three years. If it is acceptable to the Patent Office then it is published a second time as an examined (*kokoku*) specification, or B2 on the front page, or, from 29 May 1996, as a granted B2 document. If a search report is made by the Patent Office then it will be printed on the front page of a B2 at field (56). The citations are normally to other Japanese patent documents.

Formerly there was pre-grant opposition before the final registration or *toroku* stage. From January 1996 this final stage was abolished and a six month opposition period was made available after the B2 stage. Grant was obviously dependent on the applicant asking for examination, and it was normal to wait during the seven year period allowed. Some applicants are taking advantage of the ability to ask for a quick examination (if reasons are given) in which cases a B1 is published as the only specification.

The patent term from 1 July 1995 is 20 years from first filing in Japan. Pending or existing patents on that date also have 20 years. Formerly the term was 15 years from publication of the B2 provided that no more than 20 years had elapsed from the filing date.

The specification was formerly published a third time at grant after an opposition period. About 250,000 applications are published annually, and about 60,000 examined specifications. The new procedure allows for opposition to be made within 6 months of the granted B2 being published.

Utility models formerly had a similar procedure to that of the patents. The U documents are now normally published within months of the application being made as a single stage.

Specifications

From 1994 only electronic formats were used to publish Japanese specifications and paper was no longer used.

Figure 7.1 gives the front page of the unexamined application JP P2000-148694A. It is more prominently numbered as 2000-148694. This information is at the top right of the page. See Figure 7.5 for an English abstract of this specification prepared by the Japanese Patent Office in its *Patent Abstracts of Japan* database. The format of the front pages changed somewhat on 30 July 1992.

Although it may look formidable, INID codes are used in the normal way to help interpret what is what, although sometimes the details go over onto the second page. The fact that it is actually Japanese rather than another Oriental language is indicated by the country code (JP) at top left, code (19). The fact that it is an A document is given at the top in the middle at code (12). The date of publication is given at code (43) at the top right, in this case 30 May 2000. In the illustrated front page, just above the second horizontal line, to the right, is "7" with a "21" with some Japanese within brackets. The 7 means the number of claims as given on page 2. The 21 indicates the number of pages in the specification. Formerly the number of pages was often two or three but the specifications are becoming longer.

No search report details are given but there is an abstract and (usually) a drawing.

If the applicant and inventor details are for Westerners, the names are given in Western as well as Japanese characters.

The classification numbers to the right of the International Patent Classification relate to the Japanese refinement. Some information on this is in the Classification chapter on page 88.

The remainder of a specification (not just for applications) follows a set pattern. Figure 7.2 gives the first page of the same specification. The claims come first, numbered (together with Japanese characters) within brackets in the format [1], [2], etc. Formerly these were few in number, unlike Western specifications. Japanese statistics state that in 1988 the average filed patent had only 2.7 claims while by 1999 this had grown to 6.6 claims. In this case there are seven claims. They are followed by prior art and the description given in paragraphs in the format [0001], [0002], etc. The character meaning "drawing" resembles a square with an X in it: examples are just after [0003] and [0004] where drawing 25 is referred to. This is useful as, if drawing 25 looks as if it is important, then the relevant paragraphs referring to it can be sent for translation. Occasionally Western characters, such as Latin plant names or (in this example) words like "TV" and "EEPROM" (paragraphs [0006] and [0003]) will appear. The last part of the text, before the drawings, consists of numbered references to the drawings and the numbered elements within them. Derwent's useful guide (listed in the bibliography to this chapter) gives more details.

See the "Abstracts" heading for details of English abstracts and machine translations via the Internet.

(19)日本国特許庁（ＪＰ）　　(12) 公 開 特 許 公 報 (A)　　(11)特許出願公開番号

特開2000－148694

（P2000－148694A）

(43)公開日　平成12年5月30日(2000.5.30)

(51)Int.Cl.⁷	識別記号	FI		テーマコード(参考)
G06F 15/02	500	G06F 15/02	500A	5B019
	335		335E	5E501
	345		345K	5K011
3/00	654	3/00	654D	
	656		656D	

審査請求　未請求　請求項の数7　OL　（全 21 頁）　最終頁に続く

(21)出願番号　　特願平10－316460

(22)出願日　　平成10年11月6日（1998.11.6）

(71)出願人　395015319
株式会社ソニー・コンピュータエンタテインメント
東京都港区赤坂7－1－1

(72)発明者　中野　武志
新潟県北蒲原郡水原町安野町5－8

(74)代理人　100101867
弁理士　山本　寿武

Ｆターム(参考)　5B019 GA00 HD20 JA10
5E501 AA04 AA11 AA17 BA20 CA04
CB03 FA13 FB03 FB28 FB32
5K011 JA01 JA03

(54)【発明の名称】　エンタテインメントシステムの携帯用電子機器

(57)【要約】
【課題】　ゲームを実行可能な携帯用電子機器を電卓として利用する技術を提供する。
【解決手段】　プログラムの実行機能を有する親機に接続するためのインタフェースを備える携帯用電子機器であって、プログラム格納手段と、上記プログラムの実行を制御する制御手段と、上記実行されるプログラムに応じて情報を表示する表示手段と、上記プログラムを操作するための操作入力手段と、上記各手段に電源を供給する電源供給手段とを備え、親機から上記携帯用電子機器に対して電卓プログラムの実行に伴う情報が転送され、この転送された情報に基づいて上記制御手段により上記プログラム格納手段に格納された電卓プログラムを実行する。

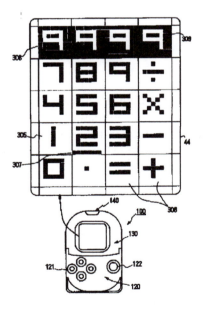

Figure 7.1. Front page of a Japanese application

Figure 7.3 gives the front page of a specification granted under the new procedure, JP 3195953 B2. Unlike the A it lacks an abstract and drawing. Frequently, as in this case, there is a search report at code (56). As in this example it usually gives only Japanese A or U citations. At the top code (24) gives the date of grant while code (45) is for the date of publication (the dates will be different). The claims are given at the bottom, in this case only four, followed by the description, numbered by paragraph [0001] etc.

Utility models before 1994 will not have a description. They are sometimes referred to as *Jitsuyo shinan koho* (their Japanese name). An example of a front page of a granted utility model under the new procedure, JP 3079074 U, is shown in Figure 7.4. They include a drawing on the front page.

CD-ROMs of all these series are issued.

The gazette

The gazette formerly consisted of the printed specifications themselves (with some additional material), namely the *Patent Application Gazette* and the *Patent Gazette*, and the *Utility Model Application Gazette* and the *Utility Model Gazette*. Japan no longer has a printed gazette giving details of its specifications.

Abstracts

Derwent Information published *Japanese Patents* (formerly *Japanese Patents Abstracts*) for chemical *kokai* specifications. The other technologies are divided into many separate subject areas within the series Alerting Abstracts Bulletin.

During 1977-93 the Japanese Patent Office published the paper *Patent Abstracts of Japan*, or PAJ. This gives English abstracts plus drawings of *most* published patent applications from 1976 by Japanese nationals. It was published in several subject sections, with each issue giving the abstracts in patent numerical order. The issues to 1993 have been reissued on IPC-based CD-ROMs as a backfile series of 99 discs, with monthly discs in numerical order being issued from January 1994. Abstracts of foreign applications were later issued in a separate backfile for 1989-1997. There are time-lags of several months before these abstracts are available.

An example of a PAJ abstract is given in Figure 7.5, where the same 2000-148694 as shown in Figure 7.1 is abstracted. Most abstracts are accompanied as in this case by a drawing but note that the drawing used was, on this occasion, different. The inventors' names at code (72) are back to front for a Westerner so Nakano Takeshi would be styled Takeshi Nakano in the West. This is a printout from the web version and includes a "legal status" which in this case (not shown) states that the "Date of request for examination" was made on 17 October 2000. The CD-ROM version does not include such status data.

This database is available on the Internet at **http://www1.ipdl.jpo.go.jp/PA1/cgi-bin/PA1INIT?**. The full Japanese text can be accessed by clicking on the "Japanese" box. By clicking on the "Detail" box when the abstract is being viewed a machine translation of the claims is generated. This is not stored and is generated "on the fly" each time a

（２）０００−１４８６９４（Ｐ２０００−１４８６９４

【特許請求の範囲】
【請求項１】　プログラムの実行機能を有する親機に接続するためのインタフェースを備える携帯用電子機器において、
プログラム格納手段と、
上記プログラムの実行を制御する制御手段と、
上記実行されるプログラムに応じて情報を表示する表示手段と、
上記プログラムを操作するための操作入力手段と、
上記各手段に電源を供給する電源供給手段とを備え、
上記親機から上記携帯用電子機器に対して電卓プログラムの実行に伴う情報が転送され、この転送された情報に基づいて上記制御手段により上記プログラム格納手段に格納された電卓プログラムを実行することを特徴とする携帯用電子機器。
【請求項２】　請求項１に記載の携帯用電子機器において、
上記プログラム格納手段に格納された電卓プログラムは、上記親機との接続が遮断された状態で実行されることを特徴とする携帯用電子機器。
【請求項３】　請求項１に記載の携帯用電子機器において、
上記接続される親機はビデオゲーム装置であり、接続された親機から上記格納手段に上記電卓プログラムがダウンロードされ、このプログラムは上記制御手段により実行されることを特徴とする携帯用電子機器。
【請求項４】　請求項１に記載の携帯用電子機器において、
上記電卓用プログラムは、上記親機に搭載されるゲームソフトを蓄積した光ディスク記録媒体に付加的に記録されていることを特徴とする携帯用電子機器。
【請求項５】　請求項１に記載の携帯用電子機器において、
上記表示手段に表示される置数キー及び演算キーのキャラクタと、計算結果の数値キャラクタとは識別可能となっていることを特徴とする携帯用電子機器。
【請求項６】　請求項５に記載の携帯用電子機器において、
上記表示手段に表示される置数キー及び演算キーのキャラクタは通常に表示され、
前期計算結果の数値キャラクタは濃淡が反転したキャラクタで表示されることを特徴とする携帯用電子機器。
【請求項７】　請求項１に記載の携帯用電子機器において、
上記表示手段の比較的小さい表示画面上に、置数キー、演算キー及び計算結果が部分的に表示され、該部分的な表示はスクロールすることにより全体を逐次表示することができることを特徴とする携帯用電子機器。
【発明の詳細な説明】
【０００１】

【発明の属する技術分野】本発明は、エンタテインメントシステムの携帯用電子機器に関し、さらに具体的には、ビデオゲーム機のような情報機器に接続可能であり、メモリカード装置等の補助記憶装置としての機能を有し、且つ、それ自体単体でも使用出来る携帯用電子機器を電卓（卓上電子計算機）として利用する技術に関する。
【０００２】
【従来の技術】ビデオゲーム機のような情報機器等の親機に挿着されて用いられている従来のメモリカード装置等の携帯用電子機器あるいは子機は、情報機器の本体（親機）と接続するためのインターフェースと、データを記憶するための不揮発性の記憶素子を備えて構成されている。
【０００３】図２５の（ａ）は、このような従来の携帯用電子機器の一例としてのメモリカード装置の主要部の構成例を示している。この従来のメモリカード１０は、その動作を制御するための制御手段１１と、情報機器等のスロット内に設けられた端子に接続するためのコネクタ１２、及びデータを記憶するための不揮発メモリ１６を備え、コネクタ１２と不揮発メモリ１６は制御手段１１に接続されている。制御手段１１は、例えばマイクロコンピュータ（以下の図中ではマイコンと略記する。）を用いて構成される。また、不揮発メモリ１６として、例えばＥＥＰＲＯＭ等のフラッシュメモリが用いられる。また、情報機器等との接続インターフェースには、プロトコルを解釈するための制御手段としてマイクロコンピュータが使われることもある。
【０００４】図２５の（ｂ）は、従来のメモリカード１０の制御手段１１における制御項目を示している。
【０００５】このように、従来のメモリカードでは、情報機器等の本体に接続するための本体接続インタフェースと、不揮発メモリにデータを入出力するためのメモリインタフェースを備えているだけであった。
【０００６】また、家庭用ＴＶゲーム装置のような従来のビデオゲーム装置は、ゲームデータ等を補助記憶装置に記憶する機能を有している。上述したメモリカード装置は、このようなビデオゲーム装置の補助記憶装置としても用いられる。
【０００７】図２６は、補助記憶装置としてメモリカードを用いる従来のビデオゲーム装置の一例を示している。この従来のビデオゲーム装置１の本体２は、ほぼ四角形状の筐体に収容されており、その中央部にビデオゲームのアプリケーションプログラムが記録された記録媒体である光ディスクが装着されるディスク装着部３と、ゲームを任意にリセットするためのリセットスイッチ４と、電源スイッチ５と、上記の光ディスクの装着を操作するためのディスク操作スイッチ６と、例えば２つのスロット部７Ａ，７Ｂとから構成されている。
【０００８】補助記憶装置として用いられるメモリカー

Figure 7.2. Claims and beginning of description of a Japanese application

(19)日本国特許庁（ＪＰ）　　　(12) **特 許 公 報**（Ｂ２）　　　(11)特許番号

特許第3195953号
（P3195953）

(45)発行日　平成13年8月6日(2001.8.6)　　　(24)登録日　平成13年6月8日(2001.6.8)

(51)Int.Cl.⁷		識別記号		ＦＩ		
Ａ２３Ｌ	1/20			Ａ２３Ｌ	1/20	Ｚ
			3 0 1			3 0 1Ｚ
∥ Ａ２３Ｇ	3/00		1 0 5	Ａ２３Ｇ	3/00	1 0 5
Ａ２３Ｌ	1/317			Ａ２３Ｌ	1/317	Ｚ
	1/325		1 0 1		1/325	1 0 1Ｚ

請求項の数4（全 5 頁）

(21)出願番号　特願平5-184421	(73)特許権者　000215969
	庭野　七郎
(22)出願日　平成5年6月29日(1993.6.29)	兵庫県西宮市甲子園春風町6−10
	(72)発明者　庭野　七郎
(65)公開番号　特開平7-8196	兵庫県西宮市甲子園春風町6−10
(43)公開日　平成7年1月13日(1995.1.13)	(72)発明者　井戸本　紀史
審査請求日　平成11年5月14日(1999.5.14)	兵庫県伊丹市池尻7丁目139番地　但馬屋食品株式会社内
	(74)代理人　100085486
	弁理士　廣瀬　孝美
	審査官　上條　肇
	(56)参考文献　特開　昭55-37161（ＪＰ，Ａ）

最終頁に続く

(54)【発明の名称】　食品素材の製造方法

1

〈57〉【特許請求の範囲】
【請求項1】　おから、澱粉類、水溶性アルギン酸塩及び水からなる混合物を、カルシウム塩を含有する凝固剤で凝固させ、凝固物を得ることを特徴とする食品素材の製造方法。
【請求項2】　おから、澱粉類、水溶性アルギン酸塩及び水からなる混合物とカルシウム塩を含有する凝固剤との凝固反応を流動下に行う請求項1記載の食品素材の製造方法。
【請求項3】　凝固物を、アルミニウム塩水溶液に浸漬して、二次凝固させる請求項1又は2記載の食品素材の製造方法。
【請求項4】　凝固物を、アルコール浸漬脱水する請求項1から3のいずれかに記載の食品素材の製造方法。
【発明の詳細な説明】

2

【０００１】
【産業上の利用分野】本発明は食品素材の製造方法に関し、より詳細にはおからを組織化させた新しい形態の食品素材を製造する方法に関する。
【０００２】
【従来技術】おから（別名、うの花、きらず）は、豆腐を製造するときの豆乳の搾り粕であり、原料大豆1kgから1.2〜1.5kg（水分80〜85%）のおからが産生し、年間75万トン（1990年の推定）もの大量のおからが副生している。従来、おからは、ごく一部が食品素材や肥料として利用されているが、大部分は家畜の飼料として用いられている。しかし、おからは水分が多く、飼料効率が低いので、畜産業者から敬遠される傾向にある。また、近年、公害などの面から畜産業者が遠隔地に移転し、運搬経費が増大し、加えて海外から安

Figure 7.3. Front page of a Japanese grant

(19) 日本国特許庁（ＪＰ）　　　(12) **登録実用新案公報** (Ｕ)　　　(11) 実用新案登録番号

実用新案登録第3079074号

(U3079074)

(45) 発行日　平成13年8月3日 (2001.8.3)　　　　　(24) 登録日　平成13年5月16日 (2001.5.16)

(51) Int.Cl.7		識別記号		FI		
B 6 5 D	85/86			B 6 5 D	5/50	1 0 1 A
	5/50	1 0 1			77/26	R
	77/26				85/38	D

評価書の請求　未請求　請求項の数5　ＯＬ　（全 14 頁）

(21) 出願番号　実願2001－199 (U2001－199)

(22) 出願日　平成13年1月22日 (2001.1.22)

(73) 実用新案権者　000003067
ティーディーケイ株式会社
東京都中央区日本橋1丁目13番1号
(72) 考案者　渡辺　和義
東京都中央区日本橋一丁目13番1号　ティーディーケイ株式会社内
(74) 代理人　100078031
弁理士　大石　皓一　（外1名）

(54) 【考案の名称】　収納体及びこれを用いた包装部材

〈57〉【要約】
【課題】　異なる方向に商品を位置決めすることが可能な収納体を提供する。
【解決手段】　箱体3に収容されることによって包装部材1を構成する収納体2であって、商品4を所定の位置に位置決め可能な凹部5を備え、凹部5が、商品4を第1の方向に位置決め可能であるとともに、商品4を第1の方向とは異なる第2の方向に位置決め可能に構成されている。このように、商品4を異なる2つの方向に位置決め可能であることから、箱体3の表面に透明なフィルムを設けて商品4を視認可能とした場合に、商品4に与えられたデザインと箱体3の表面に施されたデザインとを考慮して、商品4の位置決め方向を変更することができる。

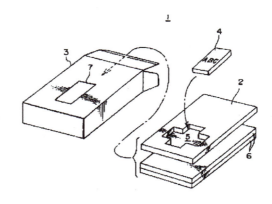

Figure 7.4. Front page of a Japanese utility model

PATENT ABSTRACTS OF JAPAN

(11)Publication number :   2000-148694

(43)Date of publication of application : 30.05.2000

(51)Int.Cl.	G06F 15/02
	G06F 3/00
	// H04B 1/38

(21)Application number : 10-316460   (71)Applicant : **SONY COMPUTER ENTERTAINMENT INC**

(22)Date of filing :   06.11.1998   (72)Inventor : **NAKANO TAKESHI**

(54) **PORTABLE ELECTRONIC EQUIPMENT FOR ENTERTAINMENT SYSTEM**

(57)Abstract:

PROBLEM TO BE SOLVED: To use portable electronic equipment, on which a game can be played as an electronic calculator by transferring information which accompanies the execution of an electronic calculator program from master equipment to the portable electronic equipment and allowing the portable electronic equipment to run the electronic calculator program stored in a program storage means by its control means according to the transferred information.
SOLUTION: This portable electronic equipment 100 as slave equipment is used as electronic equipment other than a video game device. The slave equipment 100 comprises a microcomputer

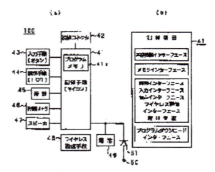

and has the control means 41, having a program memory 41a inside and a nonvolatile memory 46. The program memory 41a is stored with an operating system which controls the operation of the slave equipment. Then the control means 41 is provided with a driver which manages added functions. The electronic calculator program downloaded from the master equipment to the nonvolatile memory 46 is implemented of four arithmetical operations under the operating system.

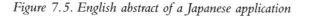

Figure 7.5. English abstract of a Japanese application

request is made. Some earlier abstracts do not seem to provide this facility. If the computer cannot translate the words then **** is generated. The translations can vary in quality but usually assist someone who knows the field of industry to decide if the specification is of interest. An example for the same 2000-148694 is shown in Figure 7.6. By clicking on the different fields at the top of the page each portion of the entire specification will be translated. The different drawings can be displayed and are referred to in the translations.

The way the web database works in response to a request for a specific, known number is that the search box defaults to assuming that you are entering a filing or "application" number. It is necessary to check the box "publication number" for an A or the box "patent number" for a B specification.

The **Esp@cenet** database also covers Japanese *kokai* but the abstracts are different.

The Patent Cooperation Treaty and Japan

Numbers within the 500,001 onwards range of the published unexamined *kokai* applications within each year are used for translations of Patent Cooperation Treaty applications that designate Japan.

Case law

The *Shinketsu koho*, the Patent Office decisions gazette, divided in 1981 into four series: patents, utility models, designs and trade marks. Patent cases dealt with by the High Court are published in an annual volume, formerly part of the *Tokkyocho koho* with the published patent applications.

Legal status data is included on the priced Patolis-e database at **http://patolis-e.patolis.co.jp**.

The British Library and Japanese patents

None of the documents in the supplementary number range for PCT specifications are held by the British Library, except for any on the CD-ROMs which are held from 1994.

The old third series of granted Japanese patents or utility models stage of publication have never been held by the British Library.

The British Library has a microfiche concordance which gives the subsequent numbers for each Japanese filing number with a single sequence for 1955-77 and thereafter annual sequences to 1993.

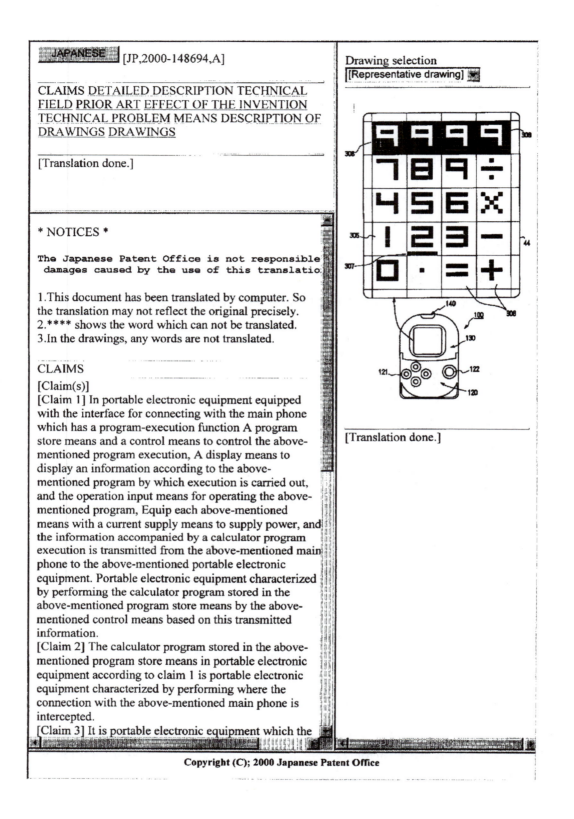

JAPANESE [JP,2000-148694,A]

CLAIMS DETAILED DESCRIPTION TECHNICAL FIELD PRIOR ART EFFECT OF THE INVENTION TECHNICAL PROBLEM MEANS DESCRIPTION OF DRAWINGS DRAWINGS

[Translation done.]

Drawing selection
[Representative drawing]

* NOTICES *

The Japanese Patent Office is not responsible damages caused by the use of this translatio

1.This document has been translated by computer. So the translation may not reflect the original precisely.
2.**** shows the word which can not be translated.
3.In the drawings, any words are not translated.

CLAIMS
[Claim(s)]
[Claim 1] In portable electronic equipment equipped with the interface for connecting with the main phone which has a program-execution function A program store means and a control means to control the above-mentioned program execution, A display means to display an information according to the above-mentioned program by which execution is carried out, and the operation input means for operating the above-mentioned program, Equip each above-mentioned means with a current supply means to supply power, and the information accompanied by a calculator program execution is transmitted from the above-mentioned main phone to the above-mentioned portable electronic equipment. Portable electronic equipment characterized by performing the calculator program stored in the above-mentioned program store means by the above-mentioned control means based on this transmitted information.
[Claim 2] The calculator program stored in the above-mentioned program store means in portable electronic equipment according to claim 1 is portable electronic equipment characterized by performing where the connection with the above-mentioned main phone is intercepted.
[Claim 3] It is portable electronic equipment which the

[Translation done.]

Copyright (C); 2000 Japanese Patent Office

Figure 7.6. Computer-generated translation of claims of a Japanese application

Internet databases

The main source is the Patent Abstracts of Japan database at
http://www1.ipdl.jpo.go.jp/PA1/cgi-bin/PA1INIT?. It contains English abstracts
and drawings of most Japanese-origin patents from 1976, particularly since 1993. It
provides automatic translations and images of the Japanese specifications for many of
them. Its coverage is limited to the *kokai*. More details are given in the "Abstracts" section.

The Patent and Utility Model Gazette DB at **http://www.ipdl.jpo.go.jp/Tokujitu/
tjsogodben.ipdl?N0000=115** provides automatic translations of specific, published
patents and utility models from 1922 onwards. It is very up to date.

The Japanese national file at the **Esp@cenet** database at **http://gb.espacenet.com**
offers an alternative database with broadly similar coverage (again only *kokai*) and images
but no automatic translations.

The priced Patolis-e site at **http://patolis-e.patolis.co.jp** offers with its English
language interface a great deal more. This includes images of patent specifications and
utility models from 1980 and data on patents from 1955 and on utility models from 1960.
This is the only electronic source for searching Japanese utility models (other than by
numbers). The site also has full legal status data.

See also the material on using the Japanese F-terms on page 88.

Contact information

Patent Office
4-3, Kasumigaseki 3-chome
Chiyoda-ku
Tokyo 100

Tel: +(81) 3 3580 9827
Fax: +(81) 3 3581 0762

Web address: **www.jpo.go.jp**

Further reading

Overseas innovations by Japanese firms: an analysis of patent and subsidiary data. R.
Belderbos, *Research Policy*, 2001, 30 (2), 313-332.

Free translation of Japanese patent documents on the Web. *Journal of the Patent and
Trademark Office Society*, G. Gooding, 2001, 83 (2), 152-155.

Conducting patent litigation in Japan: crucial considerations. G. Rahn, *Patent World*, 2001,
no 134, 20-24.

Sources of Japanese patent information. I. Schellner, *World Patent Information*, 2001, 23 (2), 149–156.

Japanese submarine patents: examined patents within a year of filing! M. O'Keefe. *World Patent Information*, 2000, 22 (4), 283–286.

Guide to reading Japanese patents. Derwent Information. London: 1995.

A guide to Japan's patent system. Japan Information Access Project. Washington, DC: 1995.

8.   PATENT CLASSIFICATION

Patent classification schemes are used to organise and index the technical content of patent specifications so that specifications on a specific topic or in a given area of technology can be identified easily and accurately.

Patent classification schemes are constructed and maintained by and for patent examiners and their primary purpose is to help the examiners in their work. When examining a patent application, the examiner needs to search a collection of patent documents to identify key relevant existing patent specifications and this task is facilitated by the use of a tailor-made classification scheme.

As part of the examination process an examiner will assign patent classification codes to the specification he is examining, so in its turn that specification becomes part of the classified collection of specifications available to examiners in the future. Therefore the classified collection of patent documents is growing constantly.

The usefulness of patent classification as a means of searching for patents information is a by-product of its primary purpose as a tool for patent examiners to test the novelty of a new patent application. Using patent classification as part of a search to identify patents in a particular field can help the non-expert searcher to focus and refine his search and produce a useful set of references. It can be particularly useful in checking the novelty of an invention but is not always so useful in other types of search such as state of the art searching.

A list of classification scheme resources on the web is at the British Library's **http://www.bl.uk/services/information/patents/othlink2.html#scheme**.

The International Patent Classification

The International Patent Classification (IPC) is currently used by over 70 patent authorities to classify and index the subject matter of published patent specifications. The IPC is maintained and is administered by the World Intellectual Property Organisation and, having first been published in 1968, is currently in its 7th edition, published in 1999 and which has been in force for usage by patent offices since January 2000. Formerly the editions were published at five year intervals but there are plans to publish every two years.

The IPC is available on CD-ROM and online as well as in hard copy.

Structure

The IPC divides patentable technology into eight Sections, A to H, as shown in Figure 8.1.

Within these sections technology is divided and subdivided to a detailed level, which allows the subject matter of a patent specification to be very thoroughly classified.

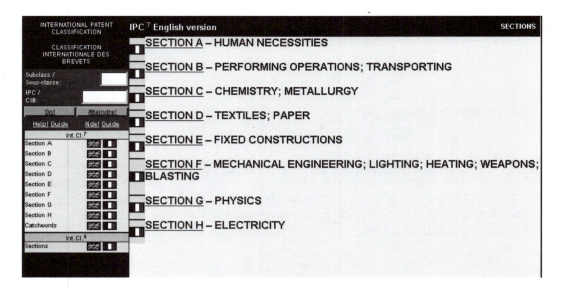

Figure 8.1. The International Patent Classification on the web at
http://classifications.wipo.int/fulltext/new_ipc/index.htm

On the web and directly reachable from the page shown in Figure 8.1 are:

- Help – for efficient use of the web pages
- The Guide – which contains useful information and advice on how the IPC should be used.
- The Catchword Index – which is a basic keyword index to the IPC schedules.
- The full detail of the text of the classification scheme, known as the schedules, can be found by clicking on the appropriate flag or section letter.

In hard copy, each of the schedules A to H is published as a separate volume. The schedules are accompanied by the following volumes: The Guide, The Catchword Index and the Concordance. The latter identifies areas in the current edition which have been revised since the publication of the first edition.

A sample page from Schedule A of the English language 7th edition of the IPC can be seen in Figure 8.2.

The IPC codes, which act as an index to the subject matter of the patent, are printed on the front page of a patent specification and are always identified by the INID code (51). There is usually a superscript numeral indicating which edition of the IPC has been used to classify the document, e.g. Int Cl[7] A01B 1/16.

The IPC is applied to the invention described in the patent specification but some patent offices also classify other (additional) information disclosed in the specification and this is listed on the front page of a document after the IPC codes classifying the invention and following a double oblique stroke symbol. Some patent offices also apply more detailed indexing codes as well as the classification codes and these have a colon rather than a stroke between the last two elements e.g. C08F 214:06. These two features are not universally applied and so cannot be used to make a comprehensive international search.

Using the International Patent Classification

Since the IPC is used by virtually all of the patenting authorities in the world (and particularly by all the authorities of the major industrialised nations) as a common means of classifying the patent specifications they publish, it is possible to carry out an international search for patents on a specific subject using the IPC as a key. However, it is a complex tool designed for an expert user group and it should always be employed with care. One of the problems with its use is that some subject approaches are not helped. For example, pharmaceuticals are classified under their structure rather than their therapeutic use.

Finding the "right" IPC classification code

Finding a classification code (or codes) upon which to base a search requires a basic grasp of how the IPC works. Taking time to browse through the Guide may help, but talking to someone who is familiar with using the IPC as a search tool will be of most value.

The Catchword Index may be a useful starting point, but it would be most unwise to search on a code identified from it without referring to the full IPC schedules to check for the context in which the code is placed and for relevant notes. The Catchword Index often proves to be inconsistent in the terms and concepts it includes.

One practical and efficient strategy for getting to the right area of the IPC schedules is to identify one or two relevant patents (perhaps via a quick keyword search of a database), see how these have been classified and then to consult that part of the IPC schedules for detailed guidance on which codes to use.

A surprising range (or scatter) of classification codes at different levels of detail and even from different areas of the IPC can be assigned to specifications forming part of a single patent family and describing the same invention, or to specifications which are closely related in terms of their technical content. This scatter may not appear to be significant, but may have considerable impact on the effectiveness of a search based on the IPC. Taking an example from the extract from the IPC schedule for agriculture, forestry, etc., shown in Figure 8.2, it is possible that a British specification describing a tong-like hand tool for uprooting weeds might be assigned the IPC code A01B 1/18, while a US specification on the same subject might be assigned the slightly less specific IPC code A01B 1/16 (hand tools for uprooting weeds). If a search for other patents on this topic were limited just to those classified at A01B 1/18, which appears to be the "right" IPC code, the US specification would not be identified. Thus the effects of the scatter become clear.

In short, the "scatter" means that it is important not to fix upon a single, very specific IPC code and to base all subsequent subject searching on that single code alone. Even if it is possible to identify an IPC classification code which appears to express perfectly the subject to be searched, it is essential to consult the full IPC schedules, to look at the hierachical context in which the code exists, to read the notes, to consider searching using a less specific code and to consider alternative codes. Note that the position of the subgroups in the hierarchy can be determined from the dots in front of the term description. This description should always be read in conjunction with the preceding term in the hierarchy having one less dot which in turn should be read with the preceding term with one less dot and so on.

Note also that the IPC codes you have identified may have changed between the editions of the IPC and as databases generally do not reclassify to the latest edition, codes from earlier editions might also need to be searched. An example is AO1B 1/24 which has the [2] suffix, meaning that it was an alteration in the 2nd edition.

IPC search tools

Searching with the IPC on a database can be simplified and speeded up by truncating IPC codes and applying Boolean logic. In the hand tool example given above it would be possible, for instance, to search for any specification assigned **either** the IPC A01B 1/16 **or** A01B 1/18 in one go. Further refinement can be achieved by searching for any specifications assigned an IPC with the stem A01B 1 and combining the results of this search with a keyword search based on the word stems Tong and Weed. With this approach careful use of the IPC can greatly enhance the scope and effectiveness of a subject search.

The format of the IPC codes used in databases is not always identical to that specified in the schedules and for example C07H 15/04 needs to be input without any spaces as C07H15/04 in **Esp@cenet**.

European classification (ECLA)

ECLA is the classification scheme applied by the European Patent Office to its internal collection of search documentation and is based on the IPC. ECLA classification codes can be used to carry out subject searches on the **Esp@cenet** database and the text of the classification schedules is published in loose-leaf format and is available on the web at **http://l2.espacenet.com/ecla/index/index.htm**. This database does not have a word index, unlike the IPC site, so the approximate class must be known. It is based on the IPC and the first stage in determining the correct ECLA codes is to find the correct IPC codes. ECLA is not only more detailed than the IPC but the European Patent Office databases which use it are consistent and also updated whenever the ECLA schedules are revised.

The **Esp@cenet** database at **http://gb.espacenet.com** contains ECLA classifications for several countries from 1920 or before (e.g. Germany, USA, France, Britain, Switzerland) although there may be gaps in the coverage, and specifications published in the last 6 months are usually not yet classified. They can be searched in the "worldwide" option and each bibliographic record contains one or more ECLA classes. These provide hypertext links to definitions in the same site given above. This means that if a patent known to be of interest is found, the ECLA class can be examined and if appropriate it can be used in the EC classification search box.

Japanese F-term classification

The Japanese Patent Office similarly has a more detailed version of the IPC. These are called the F-terms and appear on their front pages. The Patent Map Guidance website at

http://www5.ipdl.jpo.go.jp/pmgs1/pmgs1/pmgs_E provides a key. The FI box enables a search for a known IPC. This provides a code such as 2B 102, which should be clicked on. A page then explains the additional terms that can be used such as CA, which means the supply of water to livestock. The F-term box provides a definition for a known F-term.

These can then – in theory – be used in the database at **http://www.ipdl.jpo.go.jp/ Tokujitu/tjftermena.ipdl?N0000=114** to find patents with those classifications, or in the (priced) e-Patolis database at **http://patolis-e.patolis.co.jp**.

US classification

This is the scheme used by the United States Patent and Trademark Office examiners as their primary classification tool. The scheme can be used to search US patents as far back as 1790, since all the affected documents are reclassified whenever the classification schedules are revised. The schedules and an index to them can be found on the web at **http://www.uspto.gov/go/classification** and at a number of other websites. This site provides a list of relevant patents if the "P" next to the class number is clicked on. There is also a concordance between the US scheme and the IPC at **http://www.uspto.gov/ web/offices/ac/ido/oeip/taf/ipc_conc/index.html**.

The US classification is only applied to US patent specifications and cannot be used to conduct an international search. The scheme can be used to carry out searches on a number of databases which are dedicated to US patents and to search some CD-ROM products.

British classification

This is the scheme applied in parallel to the IPC to all published British patent specifications by the examiners at the Patent Office. The British classification schedules are revised and republished periodically in hard copy. Further information about the schedules is available on request from the Patent Office. The British classification cannot be used to conduct an international patent search, nor is it possible to use the British classification in an online database search, but it can be used to search British patent applications published since 1978 on the Espace UK and the ACCESS EUROPE CD-ROM databases.

Derwent classification

The classifications given above can be too detailed or inappropriate. Sometimes for example a searcher wishes to limit a field to a specific, general industrial area and avoid "false drops" by using words common to several industries. Derwent Information uses industry-based classes when compiling records for patent specifications. There are over 130 of them, from A to M, with an example being A11 which is for polysaccharides and natural rubbers. In addition Derwent has "manual codes" which are terms that are used in conjunction with IPC classes where they are not considered detailed enough. There are two series, the CPI (for chemistry and biology) and EPI (for electrical engineering). An example is A11–B09B, which is for decorative laminate production.

These classes can be used on Derwent Information's priced web or conventional online services.

Further reading

Comparing the IPC and the US classification systems for the patent searcher, S. Adams, *World Patent Information*, 2001, 23(1), 15-23.

International Patent Classification, 7th ed., 1999. World Intellectual Property Organisation. Volume 9, Guide.

The sixth edition of the IPC, B Hansson and M Makarov, *World Patent Information*, 1995, 17 (1), 5-8.

The ECLA classification system, D Dickens, *World Patent Information*, 1994, 16 (1), 28-32.

The International Patent Classification as a search tool, W. Vijvers, *World Patent Information*, 1990, 12 (1), 26-30.

A 01 B

— subsection title

AGRICULTURE

class symbol — — class title

A 01 — AGRICULTURE; FORESTRY; ANIMAL HUSBANDRY; HUNTING; TRAPPING; FISHING

subclass index — — subclass title

A 01 B — SOIL WORKING IN AGRICULTURE OR FORESTRY; PARTS, DETAILS, OR ACCESSORIES OF AGRICULTURAL MACHINES OR IMPLEMENTS, IN GENERAL (making or covering furrows or holes for sowing, planting or manuring A 01 C 5/00; machines for harvesting root crops A 01 D; mowers convertible to soil working apparatus or capable of soil working A 01 D 42/04; mowers combined with soil working implements A 01 D 43/12; soil working for engineering purposes E 01, E 02, E 21)

Subclass Index

HAND TOOLS	1/00	IMPLEMENTS USABLE EITHER AS PLOUGHS OR AS HARROWS OR THE LIKE ... 7/00
PLOUGHS		
General construction	3/00, 5/00, 9/00, 11/00	OTHER MACHINES ... 27/00 to 45/00, 49/00, 77/00
Special adaptations	13/00, 17/00	ELEMENTS OR PARTS OF MACHINES OR IMPLEMENTS ... 59/00 to 71/00
Details	15/00	
HARROWS		TRANSPORT IN AGRICULTURE ... 51/00, 73/00, 75/00
General construction	19/00, 21/00	PARTICULAR METHODS FOR WORKING SOIL ... 47/00, 79/00
Special applications	25/00	
Details	23/00	

main group symbol

main group — reference — precedence reference

1/00	**Hand tools** (edge trimmers for lawns A 01 G 3/06)
1/02	. Spades; Shovels
1/04	. . with teeth
1/06	. Hoes; Hand cultivators
1/08	. . with a single blade
1/10	. . with two or more blades
1/12	. . with blades provided with teeth
1/14	. . with teeth only
1/16	. Tools for uprooting weeds
1/18	. . Tong-like tools
1/20	. Combinations of different kinds of hand tools
1/22	. Attaching the blades or the like to handles (handles for tools, or their attachment, in general B 25 G); Interchangeable or adjustable blades
1/24	. for treating meadows or lawns [2]

subgroup symbols

guide heading

Ploughs

3/00	**Ploughs with fixed plough-shares**
3/02	. Man-driven ploughs
3/04	. Animal-drawn ploughs
3/06	. . without alternating possibility, i.e. incapable of making an adjacent furrow on return journey
3/08	. . . Swing ploughs
3/10	. . . Trussed-beam ploughs; Single-wheel ploughs
3/12	. . . Two-wheel beam ploughs
3/14	. . . Frame ploughs
3/16	. . Alternating ploughs, i.e. capable of making an adjacent furrow on return journey
3/18	. . . Turn-wrest ploughs
3/20	. . . Balance ploughs
3/22	. . . with parallel plough units used alternately

3/24	. Tractor-drawn ploughs (3/04 takes precedence)
3/26	. . without alternating possibility
3/28	. . Alternating ploughs
3/30	. . . Turn-wrest ploughs
3/32	. . . Balance ploughs
3/34	. . . with parallel plough units used alternately
3/36	. . Ploughs mounted on tractors
3/38	. . without alternating possibility
3/40	. . Alternating ploughs
3/42	. . . Turn-wrest ploughs
3/421	. . . . with a headstock frame made in one piece [2]
3/426	. . . . with a headstock frame made of two or more parts [2]
3/44	. . . with parallel plough units used alternately
3/46	. Ploughs supported partly by tractor and partly by their own wheels
3/50	. Self-propelled ploughs
3/52	. . with three or more wheels, or endless tracks
3/54	. . . without alternating possibility
3/56	. . . Alternating ploughs
3/58	. . with two wheels
3/60	. . . Alternating ploughs
3/62	. . . . Balance ploughs
3/64	. Cable ploughs; Indicating or signalling devices for cable plough systems
3/66	. . with motor-driven winding apparatus mounted on the plough
3/68	. . Cable systems with one or two engines
3/70	. . . Systems with one engine for working uphill
3/72	. . Means for anchoring the cables
3/74	. Use of electric power for propelling ploughs (electric current collectors B 60 L 5/00)

Figure 8.2. Annotated page from the 7th edition of the International Patent Classification

9 FINDING AND USING PATENT INFORMATION

This chapter discusses the options available to the novice or non-specialist searcher who wants to find and use patent information.

The source material

The primary producers of patent information are the individual issuing authorities (the national or regional patent offices or WIPO). Firstly and most obviously they publish patent specifications which:

- describe the invention in words
- index the subject matter of the invention by the use of patent classification codes
- give relevant names, dates and numbers

Alongside the specifications these authorities produce a range of gazettes, indexes and other "finding tools" which make it possible to search through the specifications.

Other organisations in both the public and private sectors collect the patent specifications, manipulate the data contained in them and make it available in a variety of formats and sometimes with a range of enhancements.

The issuing authorities also maintain status registers/files which:

- record data relating to the progress towards grant of a patent application
- record changes in the legal status of a granted patent.

The significance and usefulness of status data is dealt with further on in this chapter.

Note

Remember that the first point at which any data on a patent application enters the public domain is on publication of a specification 18 months after the priority date. Before this milestone only a handful of authorities (of which GB is the most important) make any data available and this is extremely limited in scope.

What can you achieve?

As long as you have a grasp of the main features of the patent system and an understanding of the documentation it produces, it is possible to carry out a basic patent search with some degree of confidence. You should be able to identify the work of known inventors, build up a picture of the patent portfolio of specific companies or organisations and review patents in a particular technical field.

However, problems can and do arise when someone acts on the results of a patent search without fully grasping the significance of the information which has been retrieved. There is a real danger that they might compromise their current or future rights or infringe upon the rights of other parties.

It is extremely important that anyone embarking on a patent search is aware that they should take advice from a patent agent or similarly qualified professional before acting on the search results.

Where to look for patent information

Traditionally patent searching has required access to a large library of patent specifications and associated paper and microform "finding tools". The introduction of CD-ROM products from the early 1990s onwards extended the search options. About 30 patent authorities now publish their patent specifications on CD-ROM or DVD. Some authorities (notably the USA and Japan) have stopped paper publication altogether and Germany plans to do so in the future. At the other end of the spectum a few authorities such as Italy, Israel and South Africa do not publish specifications obliging searchers to visit the national patent offices to complete their research. Authorities also continue to produce other items such as weekly gazettes and cumulative indexes in paper and on CD-ROM and these facilitate searching by name, number and classification codes (for subject searching). The traditional, library based approach to searching therefore remains a useful option for those with easy access to a substantial collection and brings with it the bonus of the help provided by experienced library staff.

"Pay to use" electronic files of patent data have been available since at least the early seventies but searching these files has been an expensive option and one which requires considerable expertise. However, the appearance of numerous free patent databases on the web in recent years has made it possible for basic patent searches to be begun online at home or in the office for little cost other than phone charges and the user's own time. This option is the one most likely to be chosen by novice searchers and it is on this approach that we will concentrate here.

Online patent files – the options

In reviewing online patent search files the most obvious distinction to be made is between those which offer free access to all users and those which offer access on a charged basis.

Free files

The most straightforward electronic files in terms of content and ease of use, the free files typically allow you to search the "front page" data of a particular set of specifications. This data covers the inventors and applicants named on the front page, the classification codes, patent numbers and dates given there, the text of the patent title and sometimes the text of the abstract.

Search results usually consist of "front page" data and a link is often provided to a facsimile of the document itself. Refinements may include the linking of patent equivalents or the provision of searchable English language titles and abstracts for foreign language specifications. There is generally no fee for searching these files and viewing and printing off copies of the specifications is normally free. However, many databases make each page of the document a separate PDF file, which makes printing a very slow process. To avoid this, software can be purchased which fools the database into supplying them all at once. The most popular options for this are PatSee from **http://www.imageapps.co.uk**, Get the Patent.com from **http://www.getthepatent.com** and PatentOrder.com from **http://www.patentorder.com**.

Priced files

These files are characterised by the extra value added to the raw patent information by the database producer. This extra value may be in the form of enhancements to the content of records for each patent/patent application and also in the provision of sophisticated search and retrieval options. The main producer of value added files is Derwent Information Ltd., which has been producing patent search tools since the mid sixties. Major patent offices such as the EPO and the French National Patent Office (INPI) are also active in the field. Traditionally these priced files have been made available by dedicated hosts such as Questel.Orbit, Dialog and STN. Each host has offered a suite of files, a sophisticated command language for searching, extensive documentation and a dedicated help desk.

Because of the cost, because some form of user agreement has to be entered into with the producer/host and because training in search languages is needed, the people who pay to use files tend to be those with a serious, long-term interest in patent searching. With the growth of web base patent files some of these files are now available on the web, typically with "fill in the blanks" search screens designed for ease of use.

Choosing a file

A great many online patent searches are unsuccessful because:

- the searcher has not chosen a file which is capable of answering the question (it does not cover the right dates, or issuing authorities, for example)
- the searcher has not read the help notes and has not followed the search protocols of the selected file, such as standard entry formats for names or numbers.

So, whatever kind of information you need, whatever your level of expertise and whatever your budget, you should find out as much as you can about about the files available to you before you begin your search. The object is to select a file which at least has the potential to answer your question at a cost acceptable to you.

Below is a basic checklist of points to consider when selecting an information source:

1. What kind of data is provided? (Are both A and B publications picked up, are family links highlighted, are facsimile images of the specifications available?)
2. What patent authorities are covered?
3. What is the extent of the backfile?
4. How often is the information updated? (Is an update loaded once a week or once a month?)
5. How up to date is the file? (What is the publication date of the most recent patent covered?)
6. What data elements are indexed and how? (Can you search for keywords in the title, for full inventor names, can you use wild cards?)

7. Are data elements such as the title translated from foreign languages?
8. What results formats are available?
9. Is there a charge for searching or for downloading results?

Unfortunately it can be difficult to find enough information to make an informed choice of database. Many free databases on the web give little or no information on exactly what they cover, their update policies, etc. The very best of them such as the official US patent database and the PCT database are updated on the day the specifications are published. Others may take weeks to load the same data. There is a list at **http://www.bl.uk/services/information/patents/keylinks.html** which comprises those files which we think will be most useful for patent searches and it will often be necessary to use more than one of them to achieve a thorough search. Above all it is important to make full use of whatever search help is provided to maximise your chances of success.

Searching for patent information

When it comes to patent searching there is no substitute for practice, underpinned by a sound understanding of patent processes and terminology. The more you use the patent files and the more you learn about search techniques the more confident and skilled you will become in constructing an effective search strategy. Most new patent searchers will want to search for patents linked to specific names (individual or corporate), for patents on specific topics, or for a combination of these two elements. What follows are guidance notes which will help you begin to search the patent databases to find this kind of information.

Name searching – key points

Personal names – search as both the inventor and applicant. If an inventor has filed an application on his own behalf or as joint applicant with a corporate body then he will be indexed both as applicant and inventor, so both fields should always be checked in a personal name search.

Personal names – how are they indexed? Are first names searchable in full, or are only initials given? If initials are used then more common surnames are guaranteed to produce a lot of "possibles" which will have to be filtered by adding in to the search strategy some limitation on subject matter or by simply scanning all the possibles in a cheap or free to view format.

Corporate names – how are they indexed? Is there any control over the way corporate names are entered so that, for example, searching for "BP" as a patent applicant will also retrieve "British Petroleum" and "BP Amoco" records? Are there standard abbreviations for terms like "University of"? If the policy is not completely clear it will be necessary to try all the options for comprehensive coverage.

How does the chosen file deal with non-standard language elements in names? Consider factors such as the transliteration of names from non-Roman scripts, the treatment of prefixes (van, de, etc.) and of accents (e.g. is ö keyed as oe?).

Trade marks/names in patent searching. Trade marks or names for patented items are not indexed in patent databases. They are usually created late on in the process of bringing a product to market, while the patent specification is drafted and filed at a very early stage in a product's life. Consequently the eventual trade name or mark is unlikely to be used in the patent specification. If you search for the trade name "Velcro" you will not retrieve the patent describing this invention, although you may locate other patents which mention its use as a means of attachment in the invention they describe.

Subject searching – key points

Define your search needs – patent files which can be searched by subject usually allow you to search by classification codes and by combinations of keywords and phrases which describe the technology being investigated. It is therefore important to start from a brief and technically accurate description of your invention or technology (how it works, what its major characteristics are). A list of any claimed benefits (of the sort found in promotional literature) is unlikely on its own to be a suitable starting point.

Search incrementally – build on what you know/discover – For an inexperienced searcher or for someone working in an unfamiliar technology the most effective strategy for beginning a patent subject search is to isolate a few relevant patents (perhaps by means of a quick search on the names of known major players) and to use these as a basis for formulating a detailed search strategy. The technical description from these patents will be a good source of subject specific vocabulary for a keyword search and the classification codes will provide a starting point for further research.

Take note of citations – If you identify one or more patents which are particularly relevant to your needs it is possible to investigate what might be termed their "family tree". This involves identifying later patents in whose search reports your "known" patent is cited as being relevant. Tracking key patents in this way will help you to follow the development and growth of a particular technology. The same technique can also be worked in reverse and the older patents cited in the search report of the "known" patent can be retrieved and examined to track the development process backwards to the earliest evidence in patents of a particular technology.

A list of the most important databases is given in the Appendix on page 107.

> ### Note
> The files used for name and subject searching are unlikely to reflect current status. Once you have identified a patent or group of patents, do not assume that the applicants named in the records you have retrieved are the current owners of the patent or that the patent is currently in force. You must carry out a separate status search for each patent (see below for details) if this data is important to your research.

Searching for status information

Misinterpretation of status data may leave you vulnerable to legal action, so you should always review it with a Chartered Patent Agent or other suitably qualified professional.

Status information comprises data on the legal standing of a patent or patent application. There are a number of stages through which a patent application passes as it progresses towards grant or refusal and if it is granted then the monopoly it confers can last for up to 20 years (longer for some pharamceuticals). During its "life" the legal status of a patent may be affected by a number of actions or events. Refusal of grant, a change of ownership, a licensing agreement or the failure to pay renewal fees will all be significant. For instance:

- To avoid the risk of infringing existing patent rights you need to check if relevant patent applications have gone to grant and if renewal fees on granted patents have been paid.
- You will need to confirm that a patent is in force before a licensing agreement is signed
- If the assets of a company are being investigated then the status of its patent applications and granted patents will be relevant.

Where to find it
Patent issuing authorities maintain status registers/files which

- record data relating to the progress towards grant of a patent application
- record changes in the legal status of a granted patent

Because decisions based upon the data can have significant commercial and legal consequences, any source of status information must be both up to date and accurate. It has long been possible to request status information from the official files maintained by national or regional patent offices by letter, fax or during a visit and a few offices now offer electronic file access. Notable amongst these are the British and European Patent Offices which both provide detailed status files free of charge and the Japanese Patent Office, which incorporates some status data into its Patent Abstracts of Japan website. In addition, status data from the larger patent offices is collated in a very few specialist, commercially produced patent databases. A charge is made for access to such files. In the absence of any other source it can be useful to visit the website of the relevant national or regional patent authority where some information on access to status data may be given. At the very least a contact for enquiries should be provided.

A list of the most important databases is given in the Appendix on page 105.

Where not to find it
The information sources used for name and subject matter patent searching are not, on their own, reliable sources of status data. Files such as **Esp@cenet** or Derwent World Patents Index only index the data which appears in published patent specifications and thus they provide a snapshot of the status of individual applications/granted patents at that moment in their life. For example, the applicant names indexed on these files will be those shown on the specification and current at the time of publication. If the monopoly rights are sold or licensed at a later date, this change of "ownership" data will not be noted by these files nor will the revocation or lapsing of a granted patent. It is vital to be aware that identifying the existence of a patent application or granted patent on such a file does not give any authoritative information on its current status.

> **Search tip**
>
> Search status files using one of the unique numbers assigned to the patent in which you are interested (application, priority or published number). If you do a name search or subject search in a status file (and not all of them will allow this approach anyway) you may identify several cases with the same applicant, inventor and title filed around the same time, between which it is hard to differentiate. It is much better to do a name/subject search on an appropriate file and then take the relevant, unique number across into a status file

Litigation, case law and licences

In general status files do not give detailed information on litigation. There are however a number of specialist files on the web which cover litigation and court decisions within a single jurisdiction. The files vary enormously in scope and coverage. One may cover patent cases only, while another will range across all forms of intellectual property and a third will cover litigation on any subject dealt with by a particular court. A list of web databases is maintained on the British Library website at **http://www.bl.uk/services/ information/patents/othlink3.html#lit**.

It is vital to take advice from a qualified professional before acting on any information retrieved from these sources.

Information on licensing agreements is very hard to come by as there is usually no legal requirement for such agreements to be registered with the patenting authority. Licensing agreements will be the concern solely of the parties entering into them and this means that there is no obvious, publicly available source for such data.

10 WHERE TO SEARCH FOR PATENT INFORMATION IN THE UK

There is a vast amount of information on the Internet and much of it is free. There is a natural tendency to think that with a fast connection and the right knowledge that is all that is needed.

The home page of the Patents Information section of the British Library is at **http://www.bl.uk/services/information/patents/home.html**. In case this web address changes the following alias will work, **www.bl.uk/patents.** It has numerous links to databases and gazettes (mostly free) as well as much other relevant information. We believe that it includes the best list of links to databases in patents, trade marks and designs anywhere on the web. The site also has links to pages giving advice about searching techniques.

There are two main problems: free sites often do not provide all that is wanted (sometimes you get what you pay for), and often it is difficult to use the resources effectively (or at all) without guidance. Novice users are strongly advised to use us or another library at least at an initial stage.

This chapter explains about the resources at the British Library and at the public patent collections elsewhere in the UK. For those elsewhere in Europe or in the USA look at the links at **http://www.bl.uk/services/information/patents/othlink2.html#lib** or else at the list of patent offices (since most have a reading room) at **http://www.bl.uk/services/information/patents/polinks.html**.

The British Library: background

The British Library's Science Technology and Innovation (STI) services are the home of the national collection's science, technology and business collection. That includes patents, in an arrangement that is unique among major countries. Elsewhere the patent offices hold the national collection of patents from around the world but in the UK the Patent Office does not hold that role (and does not have a public search or reading room). The reason is historical. The Patent Office Library was founded in 1855 to assist those who were carrying out research into technology and the patent collections were an essential part of it from the beginning. From 1964 the Patent Office Library became part of what is now the British Library.

Those wishing to use the Library must have a reader's ticket.

The British Library's collection

The core collection comprises over 47 million patent specifications from 43 patent authorities worldwide. Over half a million newly published specifications are acquired each year. At least one copy of every specification (formats can vary) is kept as it is all prior art that may be asked for.

The paper specifications are arranged by country, then by publication stage, and then by number. There is no arrangement by subject so search tools must be used to find those specifications of interest. Formerly many specifications were published on paper with others on microfiche, microfilm or aperture cards. Some countries have stopped printing on paper (Japan, USA, Austria, Switzerland) and Germany plans to stop soon. CD-ROMs or DVDs (again mainly with specifications in numerical order) are now a major part of the collection and this trend to electronic format will obviously continue. About 30 countries' patents are now taken only, or as well as on paper, in CD-ROM or DVD format.

In addition to the core collection of patent specifications, the library holds a range of related intellectual property publications including:

- Gazettes and classified abstracts
- Non-official status registers
- Inpadoc and Derwent microfiche indexes
- Books and journals on industrial property
- Case law material

At the time of writing there were seven Internet workstations plus one devoted entirely to the Derwent Innovations Index. This is a web database which enables the Derwent database to be searched for free by those in the reading rooms. Although more limited than the conventional online version it is a powerful tool. The Globalpat disks are also available enabling a search through illustrated abstracts sorted by IPC cluster. This is good for low-technology searching.

Details of our relevant holdings are given at **http://www.bl.uk/services/ information/patents/stock.html**.

The British Library: basic free reference services

There are two reading rooms for patents. Science 1 (South) houses the material relevant to Britain, that is, the British national system, the European Patent Convention and the Patent Cooperation Treaty. There is also related material. Initial searches are best begun here by asking at the British Patents Enquiry Desk. Science 1 (North) is for the foreign collections and consists mainly of US, German and French patent specifications plus the CD-ROM collection. It has the Foreign Patents Desk.

There are patents enquiry desks where staff are available to help visitors use the patent collections. This includes helping readers to begin a search by providing guidance but the searches will not be carried out for them. Written, telephone, fax and email enquiries are also dealt with by our experienced staff who will provide information on topics such as

- Status of a British patent
- Details of recent British patent filings
- Date of receipt of foreign patents
- Equivalents of a particular patent

There is however a limit to what we can provide for free, and we may have to refer you to our priced services, or to another institution.

Leaflets and brochures produced by the British Library and the Patent Office are available on request.

The British Library: reading room copy services

Reading Room Copy Services

When visiting the British Library patent reading rooms customers can copy the patent material they require using the photocopying facilities. Customers are offered a choice of using self-help photocopiers, or the While-You-Wait photocopying service, which operates from the Science 1 Patent Enquiry desk. We operate on a 30-minute turnaround service.

Self-help copying machines are activated by means of copy cards which are available for purchase at the Copy counters in Reading Room 2 South, as well as from card dispensing machines located in these and other reading rooms. Self-help copiers are located in Science reading rooms 1 and 2 South as well as 1 and 2 North. The British Library no longer supplies copies of patents to off-site customers.

The British Library: charged online services

Patents Online is a research service which can assist with a wide range of patent information enquiries: subject searches, status data, company patent profiles, patent family identification. The service is offered by a team of patent information professionals who have specialist knowledge of the documentation and information sources.

Currentscan is a watching service designed for keeping clients up-to-date with the latest patent developments in their field using search profiles based on subject data or company and inventor names.

More details are at **http://www.bl.uk/services/information/patents/poss.html**.

Contacting us

Patents Information
British Library
96 Euston Road
London NW1 2DB
Email: patents-information@bl.uk
Fax: +44 (0) 20 7412 7480

British Patents Desk	Tel: +44 (0) 20 7412 7919/20
Foreign Patents Desk	Tel: +44 (0) 20 7412 7901/2
Patents Online and Currentscan	Tel: +44 (0) 20 7412 7903
	Fax: +44 (0) 20 7412 7480

The Patents Information Network

The 13 member libraries of the Patents Information Network aim to make patent information accessible throughout the United Kingdom.

All the Network libraries maintain a patents collection which is open to the public and they offer basic enquiry services to users free of charge. Each member library has a range of other services designed to meet local needs. These may include photocopying, online database searching, patent clinics offering free consultation with local patent agents, and meetings or workshops on patents and related topics. A charge may be made for these services.

It is advisable to contact a Network library for details of its collection, services and opening hours before making a visit. Their details (including a map of their locations) are at **http://www.bl.uk/services/information/patents/pinmenu.html**.

Patents Information Network members

Aberdeen
Business and Technical Department
Central Library
Rosemount Viaduct
Aberdeen AB9 lGW
Tel: 01224 652502/505
Fax: 01224 636811
Email: bustech@globalweb.co.uk

Belfast
Patents Section
Central Library
Belfast Public Library
Belfast BT1 1EA
Tel: 02890 243233 ext. 219/265/266
Fax: 02890 332819
Email: stephenmacfarlane@hotmail.com

Birmingham
Business Insight Patents
Central Library
Chamberlain Square
Birmingham B3 3HQ
Tel: 0121 303 4538
Fax: 0121 303 1354
Email: patents.library@birmingham.gov.uk

Bristol

Commercial Library
Central Library
College Green
Bristol BS1 5TL
Tel: 0117 903 7216
Fax: 0117 903 7234
Email: business@bclcg.prestel.co.uk

Coventry

Patents Collections and Services
Lanchester Library
Frederick Lanchester Building
Coventry University
Gosford Street
Coventry CV1 5DD
Tel: 024 7688 7535/7536
Fax: 024 7688 7525
Email: lbx172@coventry.ac.uk

Glasgow

Patents Collection
Business Information Department
Mitchell Library
North Street
Glasgow G3 7DN
Tel: 0141 287 2903/5
Fax: 0141 287 2912
Email: Business_Information@cls.glasgow.gov.uk

Leeds

Patents Information Unit
Leeds Public Libraries
32 York Road
Leeds LS9 8TD
Tel: 0113 214 3347
Fax: 0113 2478 8735/9049
Email: piu@leeds.gov.uk

Liverpool

Patents Department
Business and Technology Library
Central Library
William Brown Street
Liverpool L3 8EW
Tel: 0151 233 5835/6
Fax: 0151 233 5886
Email: refbt.central.library@liverpool.gov.uk

Manchester

Technical Library
Central Library
St Peter's Square
Manchester M2 5PD
Tel: 0161 234 1987
Fax: 0161 237 5974
Email: technic@libraries.manchester.gov.uk

Newcastle upon Tyne

Patents Advice Centre
City Library
Princess Square
Newcastle upon Tyne NE99 1DX
Tel: 0191 277 4125
Fax: 0191 277 4124
Email: patents.advice@newcastle.gov.uk

Plymouth

Reference Department
Central Library
Drake Circus
Plymouth PL4 8AL
Tel: 01752 305906/7/8
Fax: 01752 305905
Email: keyinfo@plymouth.gov.uk

Portsmouth

Central Library
Guildhall Square
Portsmouth PO1 2DX
Tel: 02392 819311
Fax: 02392 839855
Email: reference.library@portsmouthcc.gov.uk

Sheffield

Business, Science and Technology Library
Central Library
Surrey Street
Sheffield S1 1XZ
Tel: 0114 273 4743/4736/4737
Fax: 0114 273 5009
Email: sheffield.cbt@dial.pipex.com

APPENDIX: ONLINE RESOURCES

This appendix gives contact details for the main services available to users in Britain, plus some details of selected databases. It must be emphasized that in many cases Internet resources, even if priced, are inadequate to sort out a problem.

The British Library website

A year is a long time on the Internet and URLs may change and new databases may emerge, so as well as using the URLs listed below you will find it useful to look at our comprehensive lists of links on the web leading off our home page alias **http://www. bl.uk/patents**. We make every effort to keep the site up to date and believe it to be the best site in the world for listing databases and gazettes on patents, trade marks and designs. The emphasis on our link pages is very much on listing free databases (some of which require registration) although some priced sites are also covered. For the more important databases there are brief explanations of scope, how to enter classifications and so on.

The main URLs for our website which are of interest to searchers are:

Keylinks to major free patent databases
  http://www.bl.uk/services/information/patents/keylinks.html
Multi-national patent databases
  http://www.bl.uk/services/information/patents/othlink2.html#multi
Single authority patent and utility model databases and gazettes
  http://www.bl.uk/services/information/patents/othlink2.html#singe
Subject-based patent databases
  http://www.bl.uk/services/information/patents/othlink2.html#sub
Other patent-related databases
  http://www.bl.uk/services/information/patents/othlink2.html#pat
Classification schemes
  http://www.bl.uk/services/information/patents/othlink2.html#scheme

In addition we have the following detailed pages:

Procedures for obtaining patent protection
  http://www.bl.uk/services/information/patents/apply.html
What is in a patent: the patent specification
  http://www.bl.uk/services/information/patents/spec.html
Searching for patents
  http://www.bl.uk/services/information/patents/search.html
  (which includes the basics of using string searching, truncation and so on)

Key information providers

Derwent Information Ltd
Derwent House
14 Great Queen Street
London WC2B 5DF
Tel: +44 (0) 20 7344 2999
Fax: +44 (0) 20 7344 2900
Email: custserv@derwent.co.uk
http://derwent.co.uk

The Dialog Corporation
3 Palace House
Cathedral Street
London SE1 9DE
Tel: +44 (0) 20 7940 6900
Fax: +44 (0) 20 7940 6800
Email: contact@dialog.com
http://www.dialog.com
http://www.askdialog.com

FIZ Karlsruhe
STN Service Centre Europe
PO Box 2465
D-76012 Karlsruhe
Germany
Tel: +49 7247 808 555
Fax: +49 7247 808 259
Email: helpdesk@fiz-karlsruhe.de
http://www.fiz-karlsruhe.de

Minesoft Ltd (UK agents for Questel.Orbit)
100 South Worple Way
London SW14 8ND
Tel: +44 (0) 20 8404 0652
Fax: +44 (0) 20 8404 0681
Email: info@minesoft.com
http://www.minesoft.com

Questel.Orbit
4 rue des Colonnes
75082 Paris Cedex 02
France
Tel: +33 (0) 1 55 04 51 00
Fax: +33 (0) 1 55 04 52 01
http://www.questel.orbit.com

STN Agency UK
c/o The Royal Society of Chemistry
Science Park
Milton Road
Cambridge CB4 0WF
Tel: +44 (0) 1223 432110
Fax: +44 (0) 1223 423429
Email: stnhlpuk@rsc.org
http://www.rsc.org

Key databases

Axiom® – http://axiom.iop.org
Priced
Database containing World Patents Index data which allows you to view the drawings as embedded images plus other services.

British Patent Status Information Service – http://webdb4.patent.gov.uk/patents
Free
The Patent Status Information Service from the UK Patent Office will provide a complete status history of GB patent applications/granted patents and post grant status data on those European patents designating GB. You must have the application number or published number before you make a search. The file cannot be searched by name or subject matter.

Delphion – http://www.delphion.com/simple
Partly priced
At the time of writing specific patent numbers can be searched to provide bibliographic data and an image of the front page free of charge. Subscription status is necessary to see the Inpadoc patent family and status data and the complete specifications. Many other options are open to subscribers.

DEPATISnet. This free database at **http://www.depatisnet.de** has an English interface. Some searching can be carried out but it is probably most useful for retrieving PDF copies of German and many other patent specifications (including all American back to 1836). Results are sorted by country.

Derwent Innovations Index – http://www.delphion.com/derwent
Priced (free access in British Library patents reading room)
Contains the same data as the Word Patents Index but accessible to those who do not have a background in information retrieval as searchers are guided by the provision of a standard search form through which it is possible to combine names, dates, keywords and classification codes.

Epoline: European Patent Register – www.epoline.org
Free
The European Patent Register from the European Patent Office provides detailed information on the status of all European and Euro-PCT patent applications. Updated daily, it can be searched by application, publication or priority number, applicant name,

inventor name and International Patent Classification codes. Decisive information such as the expected date of grant or withdrawal is available online six weeks before the legal effect date. The file does not contain comprehensive data on the post-grant status of European patents. The data given is complex in both content and presentation: non-expert users should take advice before acting on any information retrieved. There are plans to make file wrappers, the correspondence between the applicant and the EPO and other relevant papers available as Adobe Acrobat documents as they are generated once the application has been published.

ESPACENET – http://gb.espacenet.com (*other gateways available*)
Free
This is the most popular of all the patent databases and holds a vast amount of data including PDF images of many patents (back to 1877 for Germany and 1920 for several countries). The national files for each of the EPO member states generally only provide 3 years' worth of data but the worldwide option contains much more. It can be clumsy to use: the patents identified by a search are presented in the order in which each record was added to the database rather than in date, country or numerical order and there is a separate record in the hitlist for every patent specification in a patent family. A useful feature is that many records have an ECLA code (European Patent Classification), a more detailed version of the IPC. This can be used to search the files as far back as 1920. Figure A.1 shows an example of a bibliographic record.

INPADOC – *Available via the Questel.Orbit, Dialog and STN host systems and on the Delphion website (qv)*
Priced
A European Patent Office database providing information on granted patents and published applications from over 50 Patent Offices. Patents from the major authorities are covered comprehensively from the late 1960s/early 1970s. Each record consists of a patent title (in the original language, transliterated into a west European language or occasionally translated into English) and associated names, dates and numbers. The database can be searched by names (inventors or companies), dates, patent numbers and country of origin. Inpadoc does not "add value" to the records (i.e. it does not enhance the subject data available or translate all title data into English), so a keyword search is not effective. It is, however, possible to do a limited search for patents on a specific topic by using International Patent Classification codes. Inpadoc has a sophisticated patent family search facility and is generally considered to be the best online source of complete family data.

Note
Inpadoc data is also available on the free Online Bibliographic Search database (hosted by the National Informatics Centre, New Delhi) at **http://pk2id.delhi.nic.in/sera.html**. It can be difficult to use so the "Search tips" should be studied.

Inpadoc Legal Status – *Available via the Questel.Orbit, Dialog and STN host systems and on the Delphion website (qv)*
Priced
A European Patent Office database which collects current status data from 22 patent authorities worldwide including US, GB, EP and JP. The currency of the data it provides depends upon how quickly the data is supplied by the contibuting authorities.

Tetracyclic derivatives; process of preparation and use

Patent Number:	☐ US5859006
Publication date:	1999-01-12
Inventor(s):	DAUGAN ALAIN CLAUDE-MARIE (FR)
Applicant(s)::	ICOS CORP (US)
Requested Patent:	☐ WO9519978
Application Number:	US19960669389D 19960716
Priority Number(s):	WO1995EP00183 19950119; GB19940001090 19940121
IPC Classification:	A01N43/58 ; A01N43/42 ; C07D241/36 ; C07D471/00
EC Classification:	C07D471/14
Equivalents:	☐ AP556, AU1574895, AU689205, BG100727, ☐ BG62733, BR9506559, CA2181377, CN1045777B, CN1143963, CZ9602116, DE69503753D, DE69503753T, EE3231, ☐ EP0740668 (WO9519978), B1, ES2122543T, FI962927, HK1013286, HR950023, HU74943, IL112384, JP9508113T, ☐ LV11690, NO306465B, NO963015, NZ279199, PL315559, RU2142463, SG49184, SK94096, TW378210, ZA9500424

Abstract

PCT No. PCT/EP95/00183 Sec. 371 Date Jul. 17, 1996 Sec. 102(e) Date Jul. 17, 1996 PCT Filed Jan. 19, 1995 PCT Pub. No. WO95/19978 PCT Pub. Date Jul. 27, 1995A compound of formula (I) (I) and salts and solvates thereof, in which: R0 represents hydrogen, halogen or C1-6alkyl; R1 represents hydrogen, C1-6alkyl, C2-6alkenyl, C2-6alkynyl, haloC1-6alkyl, C3-8cycloalkyl, C3-8cycloalkylC1-3alkyl, arylC1-3alkyl or heteroarylC1-3alkyl; R2 represents an optionally substituted monocyclic aromatic ring

selected from benzene, thiophene, furan and pyridine or an optionally substituted bicyclic ring attached to the rest of the molecule via one of the benzene ring carbon atoms and wherein the fused ring A is a 5- or 6-membered ring which may be saturated or partially or fully unsaturated and comprises carbon atoms and optionally one or two heteroatoms selected from oxygen, sulphur and nitrogen; and R3 represents hydrogen or C1-3alkyl, or R1 and R3 together represent a 3- or 4-membered alkyl or alkenyl chain. A compound of formula (I) is a potent and selective inhibitor of cyclic guanosine 3', 5'-monophosphate specific phosphodiesterase (cGMP specific PDE) having a utility in a variety of therapeutic areas where such inhibition is beneficial, including the treatment of cardiovascular disorders.

Data supplied from the **esp@cenet** database - I2

Figure A.1   Bibliographic record from the Esp@cenet database

JAPIO

Priced

Has bibliographic data on all published, unexamined Japanese applications (Kokai Tokyo Koho) from 1976 onwards, across all patentable technology. English language abstracts began to be available from 1981 for applications with a Japanese priority. From 1991, 90% of records have had an English language abstract. The remaining 10% are those with a non Japanese priority. Applicant and inventor name, number, IPC and keyword searches can be carried out. The file is equivalent to the CD–ROM series "Patent Abstracts of Japan". JAPIO is available on Questel.Orbit and Dialog. The content seems to be about the same as the website Patent Abstracts of Japan at **http://www1.ipdl.jpo.go.jp/ PA1/cgi–bin/PA1INIT?** which provides automatic translation facilities.

Patent Full-Text and Full-Page Image Databases —
http://www.uspto.gov/patft/index.html
Free

This site is the US Patent and Trademark Office's official Internet database,
http://www.uspto.gov/patft/index.html. It provides searching of American patent
specifications from 1976, including the recently introduced applications (in a separate
database). One or two fields can be searched at a time in a quick search (if "all fields" is
selected then the full text of the specifications is searched). More complicated strategies
can be developed using the advanced search option. A field can be all fields together, or a
specified field such as applicant, keyword or the address. The "referenced by" key in the
displayed text of a specification enables later specifications where the later specification
refers back to it to be identified. Because the US Patent Office reclassifies all its
specifications each time its classification schedules are revised, it is possible to carry out a
subject search of US patents back to 1790 using the current classification.

PCT Electronic Gazette — http://ipdl.wipo.int/en
Free

Contains PCT front page data from January 1997. Although the scope is limited it is the
only free database which allows you to scroll through embedded images from the front
pages (if the image box has been marked).

PLUSPAT – *Available via the Questel. Orbit host system*
Priced

Comprehensive file of patents from 68 authorities. It unites details of all the publication
stages for an individual patent application in a single record, from unexamined publication
to examined document to granted patent. Patents from the major authorities are covered
comprehensively from the late 1960s to early 1970s. Some much earlier records are also
present. An English language title is provided for each record and English language
abstracts for the following authorities are also present: US, PCT, EP, GB, FR, DE, CH, JP
and CN. The file can be searched by ECLA classification codes.

Surf.IP.gov.sg. A free website (but with some priced options) at
http://www.surfip.gov.sg which searches many databases, including some non-patent,
simultaneously. The results and scope varies but good for South-East Asia.

World Patents Index – *Available via the Questel. Orbit, Dialog and STN host systems*
Priced

This database provides information on granted patents and published applications and now
covers the activity of around 40 Patent Offices worldwide. Coverage of all patentable
technologies started in 1974 and some technologies (e.g. chemistry) have been covered
from the mid 1960s. All the major patent offices are covered, although Japanese coverage
was limited to chemical patents and those in the electronics and engineering fields until
1994. During 1995 coverage was expanded to Japanese patents in all areas of patentable
technology. Most patent records on the database include an expanded English language
title and a comprehensive summary of the invention. It is possible to search the database
by names (inventors or companies), dates, patent numbers and country of origin. The
records can also be searched by subject using English language keywords, codes from the
International Patent Classification and codes from Derwent's own classification scheme for
patentable technology. Training in the command languages of the hosts and in the
structure of the database is necessary to make the most of what it offers.

BIBLIOGRAPHY OF PATENTS

Scope

This compilation represents a selection of publications held by the British Library which have been found useful in dealing with enquiries. Inevitably it is biased towards European materials.

The inclusion of a title is no guarantee of its usefulness to every user of this list; nor does exclusion of a title reflect on its quality. An updated (and slightly different) version of this bibliography, which also includes some material on trade marks and designs, is at **http://www.bl.uk/services/information/patents/biblio.html**. Our entire catalogue can be searched at **http://blpc.bl.uk**.

In practice it is often found that the most up to date sources of many treaties, manuals etc. are on the Internet. The British Library's extensive lists of links can be found at **http://www.bl.uk/services/information/patents.html** of which the most useful for this bibliography are probably the links to "International legislation" and "Manuals on patent procedures, databases, etc." which both run off the "Other links" site. In addition many patent offices have websites which may offer relevant material. These are listed at **http://www.bl.uk/services/information/patents/polinks.html**.

Arrangement of literature at the British Library

The unique "STI" classification is given to assist anyone looking for the item within the British Library. Generally, material less than 10 years old will be in the open access collection in the Science 1 (South) reading room at the British Library. Older material is likely to be stored elsewhere and can be ordered through the automated catalogue. Items having a location mark prefix (B) will be found in the book sequence while those prefixed (P) are in the periodical sequence. Items located at "British Patents" are at or close to the enquiry desk in the same reading room and it is best to ask the staff for assistance. Details of the STI classification used can be obtained from the enquiry desk. One "BL" location item has been included which is housed in the Humanities collection.

Abbreviations used

CPC   Community Patent Convention
EP   European Patent

EPC European Patent Office
PCT Patent Cooperation Treaty
STI Science, Technology and Innovation [the science part of the British Library]
WIPO World Intellectual Property Organisation

British and European legislation and its review

The British patent system. Report of the committee to examine the patent system and patent law. Chairman: Banks, M.A.L.
London: HMSO, 1970.
Cmnd 4407
STI Location: (B) BF 32

Convention on the patent for the Common Market (Community Patent Convention).
Luxembourg, 15 December 1975.
London: HMSO.

Proposal for a single Community Patent valid in all EEC countries but not yet in force.
STI Location: See Luxembourg Conference on the Community Patent 1975 at British Patents.

Convention on the grant of European patents (European Patent Convention). Munich, 5 October 1973. Miscellaneous No. 24 (1974)
London: HMSO, 1974.
Cmnd 5656.
STI Location: (B) BG 301

Copyright, Designs and Patent Act 1988.
London: HMSO, 1988.
Alters mainly copyright and design laws.
STI Location: (B) BF 01.

Intellectual property rights and innovation. London: HMSO, 1983.
Cmnd. 9117.
Discussion document (Green Paper) prepared by the Cabinet Office, recommending changes relating to the Patent Office, the role of Government and the abuse of rights.
STI Location: (B) BF 02.

Intellectual property and innovation.
London: HMSO, 1986.
Cmnd 9712.
The Government's White Paper containing proposals for reform of patents, designs and copyright following papers on copyright, design and performers' protection and the recording and rental of audio and video copyright material.
STI Location: (B) BF 02.

Patent Cooperation Treaty (with Regulations). Washington, DC, 1970.
London: HMSO, 1978.
Treaty Series No. 78 (1978). Cmnd 7340.
STI Location: British Patents.

Patents Act 1977.
London: HMSO, 1977.
STI Location: British Patents.

The UK Act of Parliament governing the present patent system in the UK which came
into effect on 1 June 1978.
STI Location: (B) BF 31.

Singer. R. The European Patent Convention. Rev. English text by R. Lunzer. London:
Sweet and Maxwell, 1995.
Text and commentary.
STI Location: (B) BG 301.

The texts established by the Luxembourg Conference on the Community Patent 1985.
Luxembourg: Council of the European Communities,1986.
Resolution of some of the outstanding difficulties for the CPC.
STI Location: British Patents

British and European Patent Office patent law

Aldous, W. et al. Terrell on the law of patents. 15th ed.
London: Sweet and Maxwell, 2000.
After a short history and discussion of the nature of patentable inventions, the 1977 Act is
discussed. The effect of the EPC is considered and the appendices give the texts of the
EPC, PCT, rules of the Supreme Court, articles from the Treaty of Rome, as well as the
1977 and 1949 UK Patent Acts.
STI Location: (B) BF 30.

Baxter, J. W. World patent law and practice.
London: Sweet and Maxwell; New York: Matthew Bender, 1973-.
A multinational reference work for patent practitioners arranged in subject order so that
the position in any topic can be easily obtained for a large number of countries.
Additional chapters contain details of conventions and new legislation. Loose-leaf,
updated about three times each year.
STI Location: (B) BH 30.

Butterworths intellectual property handbook. 4th ed. Consulting editor, J. Phillips.
London: Butterworths, 1999.
Reprints numerous laws and statutory instruments.
STI Location: (B) BF 01.

Cawthra, B.I. Patent licensing in Europe. 2nd ed.
London: Butterworths, 1986.
Traces recent developments of the patent licensing system in Europe citing significant
decisions of the European Court and provides commentary on clauses in licensing

agreements related to EEC countries giving some comparison with American law.
STI Location: (B) BH 362.

Chartered Institute of Patent Agents. CIPA guide to the Patents Act 1977. 4th ed.
London: Sweet and Maxwell, 1995-.
Reproduces the UK Act section by section, with commentary. Rules made under the Act
and other statutes are added as an appendix. Supplements provide comments on cases and
more recently published rules.
STI Location: (B) BF 30.

Chartered Institute of Patent Agents. European patents handbook. 2nd ed.
London: Oyez Longman, 1988-.
Contains over 350 pages of commentary and reproduces EPC, CPC, PCT texts and
guidelines for examination under the EPC and PCT. Loose-leaf, updated periodically.
STI Location: (B) BG 30.

Patent Cooperation Treaty Handbook. London: Chartered Institute of Patent Agents,
1997- .
Explains how to use the Treaty with updates of revisions etc.
STI Location: (B) BG 303.

Phillips, J. and Firth, A. Introduction to intellectual property law. 3rd ed.
London: Butterworths, 1995.
Readable introduction to basic intellectual property principles.
STI Location: (B) BF 00.

Robertson, R. Legal protection of computer software.
London: Longman, 1990.
Covers the protection available for software by means of patents as well as by laws of
copyright, trade secrets and trade marks. Also covers remedies.
STI Location: (B) BF 191.

Singer, R. The European Patent Convention. Rev. English text by R. Lunzer.
London: Sweet and Maxwell, 1995.
Text and commentary.
STI Location: (B) BG 301.

The taxation of patent royalties, dividends, interest in Europe.
Amsterdam: International Bureau of Fiscal Documentation. 1963-. A Guide to 18
countries, loose-leaf updated about once a year.
STI Location: (B) BH 12.

Walton, A.M. et al. Patent law of Europe and the United Kingdom.
London: Butterworths, 1981-2.
Contains commentary on the UK 1949 and 1977 Acts, EPC, CPC and PCT and
reproduces the UK statutes, the EPC, CPC and the PCT. Other sections contain
information on forms and precedents, practice etc.
STI Location: (B) BG 30.

United States patent law

Chisum, D.D. Patents: a treatise on the laws of patentability, validity and infringement.
New York: Matthew Bender, 1978.
Highly detailed analysis of American laws with extensive reference to court cases. Includes an index of the cases referred to. Loose-leaf, updated periodically.
STI Location: (B) BL 36.

Lipscomb, E.B. Lipscomb's Walker on patents, 3rd ed.
Rochester, N.Y.: Lawyers Co-operative Publishing, 1984-.
Discusses designs, plants etc. as well as patents with extensive reference to court cases. Includes an index of the cases referred to. Bound, with loose-leaf updates periodically.
STI Location: (B) BL 30.

United States Code Annotated, Title 35, Patents.
St Paul, Minn.: West Publishing, 1984.
Includes text of Patent Office regulations, etc. and PCT matters. Extensive references to court cases.
STI Location: (B) BL 31.

German patent law

Gebrauchsmustergesetz 1987. Ed. by H-F. Klunker et al.
Cologne: Heymanns, 1986.
Consists of German text, with parallel English translation, of the German Utility Model Act 1987.
STI Location: (B) BJ 29.

Industrial property laws of the Federal Republic of Germany: patent, utility model, trademark, design. Ed. by V. Vossius and U.C. Hallmann. 2nd ed.
Munich: Wila, 1985.
Consists of texts of the laws.
STI Location: (B) BJ 25.

Krasser, R. Lehrbuch des Patentrechts. 4th ed.
Munich: Beck'sche, 1986.
Discusses, in German, German and European Patent Office laws.
STI Location: (B) BJ 29.

Stockmair, Wilfried. The protection of technical innovations and designs in Germany: obtainment, exploitation, enforcement. 2nd ed.
Munich: C.H. Beck, 2001.
Outlines German patent and utility model laws.
STI Location: (B) BJ 25.

Japanese patent law

Patent Office. Examination manual for patent and utility model in Japan.
Tokyo: AIPPI, 1986-.
In English. A guide to examining procedure. Loose-leaf, updated periodically.
STI Location: (B) BK 04.

Patent Office. Guide to industrial property in Japan.
Tokyo: Patent Office, 1994.
In English. A useful guide to application and examination procedures in Japan.
STI Location: (B) BK 00.

Obtaining patent protection

Bissell, P. and Barker, G. A better mousetrap: a guide for innovators. 4th ed.
Halifax: Wordbase Publications, 1995.
Short but well-presented guide to exploiting an invention.
STI Location: (B) BF 48.

Greene, Ann Marie. Patents throughout the world.
New York: Trade Activities Inc., 1981-.
Covers the procedures of over 150 countries and includes sections on international
conventions; entries are fairly brief but are updated about three times a year. Loose-leaf
format.
STI Location: British Patents and Foreign Patents.

Grubb, P.W. Patents for chemicals, pharmaceuticals and biotechnology.
Oxford: Oxford University Press, 1999.
A guide for the chemist inventor providing sections on patenting, the history of patents
and the effect of law in the EEC, USA, Comecon and developing countries. It also
contains a glossary of patent terms.
STI Location: (B) BH 30.

Guidelines for examination in the European Patent Office.
Munich: EPO, 1992.
Contains sections on formalities, search, substantive examination, opposition, etc. Loose-
leaf, updated periodically.
STI Location: British Patents.

Katzarov, K. Manual on industrial property. 9th ed.
Geneva: Katzarov, 1981-.
Provides, in two volumes, the main features of industrial property legislation and
procedure in more than 150 countries; contains a section on international conventions.
Loose-leaf format, updated periodically.
STI Location: (B) BH 00.

Manual for the handling of applications for patents, designs and trade marks throughout the world.
Amsterdam: Manual Industrial Property BV, 1936-.
Commonly referred to as "The Dutch Manual". Loose-leaf, updated by supplements, in more detail than the previous entry but updated less frequently, about once a year.
STI Location: British Patents; Foreign Patents

Manual of patent practice in the UK Patent Office. 4th ed.
London: Patent Office, 2000.
Reproduces, with extensive commentary for the benefit of staff interpreting the law, the text of the 1977 Patents Act.
STI Location: British Patents.

Newton, D. et al. The inventor's guide: how to protect and profit from your idea. London: The British Library/Gower, 1997.
Aimed at the individual inventor who lacks the resources of professionally employed inventors, it covers information sources, acquiring a patent, developing an invention, professional services, finance, marketing, designs, addresses and publications.
STI Location: (B) BF 48.

PCT applicant's guide.
Geneva: WIPO, 1991-.
Information on how to file applications, processing procedures, etc. in three volumes. Loose-leaf, updated periodically.
STI Location: British Patents.

Shaw, L. The practical guide for people with a new idea. Rev. ed.
Birmingham: L. Shaw, 1996.
A brief guide to the protection of intellectual property for the inventor wishing to exploit his idea.
STI Location: (B) BF 48.

Patents as information

Handbook on industrial property information and documentation.
Geneva: WIPO, 1990-.
In English and French. Contains sections on PCT minimum documentation; standards for patent documentation; International Patent Classification; PCT; kinds of patent publications (with samples of front pages); storage and copying (including a catalogue of microfilms); and access to patent documentation (listing many commercial and other services available). Loose-leaf format, two volumes, periodically updated.
STI Location: British Patents; Foreign Patents.

Manual of online search strategies: Vol. 2, Business, law, news & patents. 3rd ed. Ed. C J Armstrong, J A Large.
London: Bookpoint, 2001.
BL Location: 2719.k.2679.

Newton, D. How to find information: patents on the Internet.
London: British Library, 2000.
Explains in detail how to use Internet sources to find information on patents, especially databases.
STI Location: (B) BG 36.

Rimmer, B.M. International guide to official industrial property publications. 3rd ed.
London: British Library, 1992.
Describes the specifications, gazettes and other publications of 40 patenting authorities with additional information on designs and trade marks.
STI Location: (B) BH 39.

World Patent Information.
Oxford: Elsevier Science, 1979–.
Quarterly.
Contains articles on patent searching and related topics and reviews of new books and articles in periodicals.
STI Location: (P) BH 39 – E(l).

Invention; patenting history

American enterprise: nineteenth-century patent models.
New York: Cooper-Hewitt Museum, 1984.
Illustrates numerous models, arranged by topic, from the museum's collection.
STI Location: (B) BF 482.

Baker, R. New and improved.
London: British Library Publications, 1976.
Illustrated descriptions of 363 significant patented inventions dating from 1691 to 1971, e.g. typewriter, Portland cement, jet engine. Includes patent numbers.
STI Location: (B) BF 482.

Davenport, Neil. The United Kingdom patent system.
Havant: Kenneth Mason, 1979.
A compact summary which contains much detail illustrating the development of the UK patent system over 400 years up to the 1977 Act. The bibliography includes a list of statutes and rules, law reports and official publications with reports of Committees of Enquiry.
STI Location: (B) BF 46.

Desmond, K. The Harwin chronology of inventions, innovations, discoveries.
London: Constable, 1987.
Lists several thousand inventions in a chronological arrangement.
STI Location: (B) BF 48.

Dulken, S. van. British patents of invention, 1617-1977: a guide for researchers.
London: British Library, 1999.
A guide for those researching either the history of the British patent system or looking for British patents by number, name or subject.
STI Location: (B) BF 46.

Dulken, S. van. Inventing the 19th century: The great age of Victorian inventions.
London: British Library, 2001.
Illustrates and discusses 100 patented Victorian inventions.
STI Location: (B) BF 481.

Dulken, S. van. Inventing the 20th century: 100 inventions that shaped the world.
London: British Library, 2000.
Illustrates and discusses 100 patented inventions.
STI Location: (B) BF 482.

Dutton, H.I. The patent system and inventive activity during the industrial revolution,
1750 – 1852. Manchester: Manchester University Press, 1984.
An assessment of the part played by patents in the development of industry in Britain.
Part I discusses the patent institution – the system, law, courts, and patent agents. Part II
reviews the economics of patents and invention. Contains an extensive bibliography.
STI Location: (B) BF 46.

Giscard d'Estaing, V.- A. The world almanac book of inventions.
New York: World Almanac Publications, 1985.
Lists 2000 inventions by subject.
STI Location: Centre Desk (B) BF 482.

Jewkes, J. et al. The sources of invention.
London: Macmillan, 1969.
A frequently cited book about inventors and inventions including more than 50 case
histories of important inventions, e.g. automatic transmission, DDT, transistors.
STI Location: (B) BF 48.

Macleod, C. Inventing the Industrial Revolution: the English patent system 1660-1800.
Cambridge: CUP, 1988.
A detailed study of British patenting patterns before 1800. Includes a lengthy bibliography.
STI Location: (B) BF 46.

Newton, D.C. New manufactures within this realm.
London: British Library, Science Reference Library, 1985.
A chronological list of the principal changes affecting the law on patents in the UK since
the Statute of Monopolies 1624.
STI Location: (B) BF 46.

The Paris Convention for the Protection of Industrial Property 1883 to 1983.
Geneva: WIPO, 1983.
An account of the history of the Paris Convention and the evolution of the governing
secretariat and WIPO.
STI Location: (B) BG 205.

Robertson, P. The New Shell book of firsts. 3rd ed.
London: Headline Books, 1994.
STI Location: British Patents.

Case law

Case law of the Boards of Appeal of the European Patent Office 1987-1992. Ed. by the European Patent Office, Directorate-General 3 (Appeals).
Munich: European Patent Office, 1993.
STI Location: (B) BF 06.

Chartered Institute of Patent Agents. European patents sourcefinder.
London: Longman, 1988-.
Gives details, with indexes, of European Patent Office decisions. Updated at intervals.
STI Location: British Patents.

Fleet Street reports of industrial property cases from the Commonwealth and Europe (previously Fleet Street patent law reports).
London: European Law Centre. 1963-.
Commercially published edited transcripts of selected proceedings in various courts. Some Patent Office decisions are included and also, since 1973, decisions of the European Court and European Commission.
STI Location: British Patents.

Fletcher-Moulton, H. Digest of the patent, design, trade mark and other cases.
London: Patent Office, 1959.
Digests of cases between 1883 and 1955 published in the last entry in this section with indexes by topic and party. Effectively continues M. Fysh's The intellectual property citator, and continues P.A. Hayward's Hayward's patent cases 1600-1883.
STI Location: British Patents.

Fysh, M. The industrial property citator.
London: European Law Centre, 1982.
Indexes decisions in published Commonwealth law reports from 1955 to 1981 by topic and party. Effectively continues previous titles and continued by the next title.
STI Location: British Patents.

Fysh, M. The intellectual property citator 1982-1996.
London: Sweet and Maxwell, 1997.
Indexes decisions in Commonwealth and European Patent Office law reports by topic and party.
Continues the previous title.
STI Location: British Patents.

Hayward, P.A. Hayward's patent cases 1600-1883.
Abingdon: Professional Books, 1987.
Reprints and indexes in 11 volumes published patent decisions from various sources. Effectively continued by H. Fletcher-Moulton's Digest of the patent, design, trade mark and other cases.
STI Location: British Patents.

Intellectual property decisions.
Sudbury: Centre for Legal and Business Information, 1978-.
10 issues p.a.

Provides alerting abstracts of most of the significant decisions in British and European courts in the field of intellectual property.
STI Location: British Patents.

Reports of patent, design and trade mark cases.
London: Sweet and Maxwell, 1884-.
An officially printed series compiled by a legal editor giving the judgements delivered by British courts in selected cases.
STI Location: British Patents.

Current reviews

European intellectual property review.
Oxford: ESC Publishing, 1978-.
Monthly.
Articles of current interest and a section on recent legal cases, legislation and news items, country by country.
STI Location: (P) BH 00 – E(6).

World intellectual property report.
Washington, DC: BNA, 1987-
Monthly.
News on international developments in legislation, important decisions, etc.
STI Location: (P) BH 00 – E(15).

Statistics

Industrial property statistics.
Geneva: WIPO, 1976-94.
Annual.
Provides statistics on all sections of industrial property activity in WIPO member countries. See the website **http://www.wipo.int/ipstats/en** for partial later coverage.
STI Location: (P) BH 10 – E(l).

100 years' protection of industrial property: statistics.
Geneva: WIPO, 1983.
Synoptic tables on patents, trade marks, designs, utility models and plant varieties 1883-1982.
STI Location: (P) BH 10 – E(2).

Dictionaries and glossaries

The dictionaries held in the (B) AA sequence are in the Science 2 (South) reading room.

Berson, A.S. et al. English–Russian patent dictionary.
Moscow: Soviet Encyclopedia Publishing House, 1973.
Includes lists of expanded and translated abbreviations and translations of titles of official gazettes.
STI Location: (B) AA 145.

Industrial property glossary.
Geneva: WIPO.
A series of publications giving translations of about 300 main terms some of which are subdivided into related terms:
English-French-Portuguese (1980)
English-French-Russian (1980)
English-French-Chinese (1981)
English-French-German (1982)
STI Location: (B) AA 161.

Kase, Francis J. Dictionary of industrial property terms: English, Spanish, French, German.
Alphen van den Rijn: Sijthoff and Noordhoff, 1980.
STI Location:(B) AA 161.

Klaften, B., Wittman, A. and Klos, J. Worterbuch der Patentfachsprache = Patent terminological dictionary, English-German, German-English. 5th ed.
Munich: Wila, 1986.
Contains a supplement of terms relating to patent drawings.
STI Location: (B) AA ll9(GER).

Russell, Robert W. (compiler). Patents and trademarks in Japan. 3rd ed.
Tokyo: Russell, 1974.
More than 700 Japanese terms transliterated and arranged in alphabetical orders of English meaning with a full explanation of their significance in Japanese law.
STI Location: (B) BK 00.

Szendy, Gyorgy. Worterbuch des Patentwesens in funf Sprachen. 2nd ed.
Dusseldorf, VDI Verlag, 1985.
German, English, French, Spanish, Russian.
STI Location: (B) AA 161.

Ueki, Eikichi. Six-Languages dictionary of industrial properties.
Tokyo: Patent Data Centre, 1979.
Japanese, English, French, German, Russian, Spanish.
STI Location: (B) AA 161.

Uexkull, J-Detlev Von, and Reich, H.J. Worterbuch der Patentpraxis.
Koln: Heymanns, 1983.
German-English, English-German.
STI Location: (B) AA 119.

Work, H., et al. English-Russian-Estonian patent dictionary.
Tallinn: Valgus, 1976.
Translations are given for words, associated terms and phrases encountered in connection with patents.
STI Location: (B) AA 161.

GLOSSARY OF PATENT TERMS

This glossary of definitions gives "simplified" rather than "official" definitions. Some of these words are defined in somewhat different forms across the world, and this list favours British usage. The sources listed in the bibliography should be consulted for variations. All the words in bold are defined in this list.

Anticipation. When the **prior art** indicates that a patent application lacks **novelty**.

Applicant. The person or corporate body that applies for the **patent** and intends to "work" the invention, i.e. to manufacture or licence the technology.

Assignee. In the USA, the person or corporate body who acquires the rights to manufacture or license an invention from the inventor, often by contingency contracts.

Claims. The definition at application of the monopoly that the **applicant** is trying to obtain for the invention, or the actual monopoly that is given at **grant**.

Convention. "Filing by the Convention" means obeying the rules established by the 1883 Paris Convention. This usually has the connotation of filing foreign applications within 12 months of the **priority date** application.

Disclosure. The first publication of details of an invention. This may be deliberately revealed outside the patent system to make the invention unpatentable.

Disposal. A term used in some countries such as the USA to mean that an application has been resolved by being withdrawn, rejected or granted. It can also have the connotation of being rejected only.

Equivalent. These are **specifications** published by different patent offices for the same invention. Together they form the **patent family**.

Examination. See **Preliminary examination** and **Substantive examination**.

Expiry. The date when a **patent** has run its full **term** in a country and is no longer protected there. Can also be used to mean **lapsing**.

File wrapper. A term often used to mean the correspondence and other papers relating to a particular patent application.

Grant. A temporary right given by a patent office to an **applicant** to prevent anyone else from using the technology defined in the **claims** of a **patent**.

In force. A term used for a **patent** that is currently protected in a particular jurisdiction (as opposed to one that has **lapsed** or **expired**).

Infringement. An alleged or actual manufacture or import of an invention currently protected by a patent.

Interference. Proceedings before the US Patent Office to establish who has prior rights in an invention. The USA is the only country to recognise the date of invention rather than the date of priority filing as the crucial date.

Lapsing. The date when a patent is no longer protected in a country or system due to failure to pay renewal fees. Often, however, the patent can be reinstated within a limited period.

Maintenance fees. The American term for **Renewal fees**.

Novelty. The concept that the **claims** defining an invention in a patent application must be totally new. Most patent offices define this as not being revealed or publicly available anywhere in the world before the **priority date** but in the USA novelty is normally determined by the date of invention.

Obviousness. The concept that the **claims** defining an invention in a patent application must not be a predictable improvement on what has been done or published before the **priority date**.

Open to public inspection (OPI). The date when a patent application was first made available to the public to see (this may be by making them available at the patent office rather than by publishing them). This is normally not less than 18 months from the **priority date** but patent offices vary in their treatment.

Opposition. A request to the patent office by an opposing party that an application should be refused, or that a granted patent should be annulled.

Patent. Document defining rights conferred by the **grant**, but often (misleadingly) used to mean any published **specification**.

Patent family. All the **equivalents** of a **specification**.

Patent Office. The public body which receives and grants patents in each country.

Patentability. The ability of an invention to satisfy the legal requirements for obtaining a **patent**, including **novelty**. Some types of inventions, e.g. computer software and life-forms, may be unpatentable in many countries.

Patentee. In the USA, the inventor in a specification, who has the theoretical rights to the invention, although they are often signed over to an **assignee**.

Pending. When a patent office has not yet decided whether to **reject** or to **grant** a patent application, and it has not been **withdrawn**.

Petty patent. See **Utility model**.

Preliminary examination. The initial study of an application by a patent office, which in Britain involves checking that the **specification** is properly set out, and preparing a **search report**.

Prior art. Previously used or published technology, that may be referred to in an application.

Priority date. The initial date of filing of a patent application, normally in the applicant's domestic patent office. This date is used to help determine the novelty of an invention.

Registration. The act of making a **grant** of a **patent** by obtaining fees rather than by checking for **novelty** etc. by using a **substantive examination**.

Rejection. When a patent office decides to refuse a patent application on one or more grounds.

Renewal fees. Payments that must be made by the **applicant** to keep the **patent in force** and prevent it from **lapsing**. Called maintenance fees in the United States.

Restoration. Restoring a **patent** to protection after it has apparently **lapsed** by error.

Revocation. Nullifying the protection given to a patent because of e.g. lack of novelty.

Search report. The list of citations of published **prior art** documents prepared by the patent office examiner in checking the **novelty** of a patent application.

Specification. The description, drawings and claims of an invention prepared to support a patent application. The term does not imply that the invention is necessarily new or was ever protected.

Status. The legal standing of a patent or patent application i.e. pending, lapsed, still protected.

Substantive examination. The examination by the patent office examiner of a patent application to determine whether a patent should be granted. Some countries do not do this and merely use **registration** provided that the fees are paid.

Supplementary Protection Certificate (SPC). The name given in Europe to an extension of term given to a pharmaceutical or plant protection patent as a result of losing part of the term while awaiting permission to use the product.

Term of patent. The maximum number of years that the monopoly rights conferred by the **grant** of a **patent** may last.

Utility model. A kind of patent available in some countries which involves a simpler inventive step than that in a patent. Also known by other names such as a petty patent or short-term patent.

Withdrawn. The permanent abandonment of a patent application either before or after publication. Often used to mean rejection by the patent office as well as withdrawal by the applicant.

INID AND COUNTRY CODES

The World Intellectual Property Organization (WIPO) is responsible for standards within the intellectual property area. These are known as "ST" standards together with a number, and are used by most countries as appropriate in their documents, normally on the front pages. They help to harmonise the usage and appearance of patent specifications and related material, and provide a means of conveying information without using foreign languages or scripts.

The official full version of Standard 9, *Recommendations concerning bibliographic data on and relating to patents and SPCs* is given on WIPO's Internet site at **http://www.wipo.org/scit/en/standards/pdf/st_9.pdf** as an Adobe Acrobat document.

ST.9 uses numbers to identify bibliographic elements in patent specifications, normally on the front pages of images of the specifications. They are only sometimes given in numerical order on patent specifications. They are nicknamed "INID codes" after "internationally agreed numbers for the identification of bibliographic data".

The official full version of Standard 3, *Recommended standard on two-letter codes for the representation of states, other entities and intergovernmental organizations* is given at **http://www.wipo.int/scit/en/standards/pdf/st_3.pdf** as an Adobe Acrobat document.

ST.3 codes are used to identify countries, territories and regional systems in industrial property, and are heavily used on specifications on front pages and in search reports, and often within the description. They are also used by multi-national databases. They are nicknamed "country codes".

Shortened versions of the INID codes, without notes, are given below. They are not authoritative definitions. This is followed by the country codes.

INID codes

(10)   Identification of the publication

(11)   Number of the publication
(12)   Kind of publication
(13)   Kind of document code (according to ST.16)
(15)   Patent correction information
(19)   Country code (according to ST.3), or other identification, of the country of publication

(20)   Local filing details

(21)   Number given to the application
(22)   Date of making application
(23)   Other date(s) of filing, such as of complete application

(24) Date from which industrial property rights may have effect
(25) Language in which the published application was originally filed
(26) Language in which the application is published

(30) Priority details

(31) Number assigned to priority application
(32) Date of filing of priority application
(33) Country in which priority application was filed
(34) Priority filings under regional or international arrangements. At least one Paris Convention member state must be named.

(40) Date of publication

(41) Date of making available to the public by viewing, or copying on request, an unexamined specification which has not yet been granted
(42) Date of making available to the public by viewing, or copying on request, an examined specification which has not yet been granted
(43) Date of publication by printing of an unexamined specification which has not yet been granted
(44) Date of publication by printing of an examined specification which has not yet been granted
(45) Date of publication by printing of a granted patent
(46) Date of publication by printing of the claim(s) only
(47) Date of making a granted patent available to the public by viewing, or copying on request
(48) Date of issuance of a corrected patent document

(50) Technical information

(51) International Patent Classification
(52) Domestic or national Classification
(53) Universal Decimal Classification
(54) Title of the invention
(55) Keywords
(56) List of prior art documents
(57) Abstract or claim
(58) Field of search

(60) Reference to other legally related domestic document(s)

(61) Related by addition
(62) Related by division
(63) Related by continuation
(64) Related by reissue
(65) Related by being the same application
(66) Related by filing after abandonment
(67) Related by filing as a utility model after filing as a patent
(68) Related by filing for a Supplementary Protection Certificate (SPC)

(70) Identification of parties

(71)   Name of applicant
(72)   Name of inventor
(73)   Name of grantee
(74)   Name of attorney or agent
(75)   Name of inventor who is also applicant
(76)   Name of inventor who is also applicant and grantee

(80) - (90) Identification of data related to International Conventions and to legislation with respect to SPCs

(81)   Designated State(s) according to the Patent Cooperation Treaty (PCT)
(83)   Information relating to deposit of microorganisms under e.g. the Budapest Treaty
(84)   Designated contracting states under regional patent conventions
(85)   Date of supply of the international patent application to the national patent office
(86)   Filing data of the international application
(87)   Publication data of the international application
(88)   Date of deferred publication of the search report
(89)   Date of the original application under the CMEA (inventors' certificates)

(91)   Date on which an international document filed under the PCT fails to enter the national or regional phase
(92)   For an SPC, number and date of the first national authorisation to place the product on the market
(93)   For an SPC, number, date and where applicable country of origin of first authorisation to place the product on the market within a regional economic community
(94)   Calculated date of expiry of the SPC or the duration of the SPC
(95)   Name of the product protected by the basic patent and the SPC
(96)   Filing date of the regional application
(97)   Publication date of the regional application

Country codes

Old codes formerly used are also given as they may be found on old specifications. IB is an informal code used for International Bureau by WIPO within the filing number on PCT specifications filed directly through Geneva.

Regional and international organisations are given in a separate section at the end.

The Internet version includes no-longer used codes and a code-to-country concordance.

Afghanistan	AF
Albania	AL
Algeria	DZ
Andorra	AD
Angola	AO
Anguilla	AI
Antigua and Barbuda	AG
Argentina	AR

Armenia	AM
Aruba	AW
Australia	AU
Austria	AT (OE before 1978)
Azerbaijan	AZ
Bahamas	BS
Bahrain	BH
Bangladesh	BD
Barbados	BB
Belarus	BY
Belgium	BE
Belize	BZ
Benin	BJ
Bermuda	BM
Bhutan	BT
Bolivia	BO
Bosnia and Herzegovina	BA
Botswana	BW
Brazil	BR
British Virgin Islands	VG
Brunei Darussalam	BN
Bulgaria	BG
Burkina Faso	BF (HV before 1984)
Burundi	BI
Cameroon	CM
Canada	CA
Cape Verde	CV
Cayman Islands	KY
Central African Republic	CF
Chad	TD
Chile	CL
China	CN
Colombia	CO
Comoros	KM
Congo, Democratic Republic of (former Zaire)	CD (ZR before 1997)
Congo, Republic of	CG
Costa Rica	CR
Croatia	HR
Cuba	CU
Cyprus	CY
Czech Republic	CZ
Czechoslovakia, former	CS
Denmark	DK
Djibouti	DJ
Dominica	DM
Dominican Republic	DO

Ecuador	EC
Egypt	EG
El Salvador	SV
Equatorial Guinea	GQ
Eritrea	ER
Estonia	EE
Ethiopia	ET
Falkland Islands	FK
Fiji	FJ
Finland	FI
France	FR
Gabon	GA
Gambia	GM
German Democratic Republic, former	DD
Germany	DE (DT before 1979)
Ghana	GH
Gibraltar	GI
Greece	GR
Grenada	GD
Guatemala	GT
Guernsey	GG
Guinea	GN
Guinea-Bissau	GW
Guyana	GY
Haiti	HT
Honduras	HN
Hong Kong Special Administrative Area	HK
Hungary	HU
Iceland	IS
India	IN
Indonesia	ID
Iran	IR
Iraq	IQ
Ireland	IE
Israel	IL
Italy	IT
Ivory Coast	CI
Jamaica	JM
Japan	JP (JA before 1979)
Jordan	JO
Kampuchea	KH
Kazakstan	KZ
Kenya	KE
Kiribati	KI
Korea, Democratic People's Republic of	KP

Korea, Republic of	KR
Kuwait	KW
Kyrgyzstan	KG
Laos	LA
Latvia	LV
Lebanon	LB
Lesotho	LS
Liberia	LR
Libya	LY
Liechenstein	LI
Lithuania	LT
Luxembourg	LU
Macau	MO
Macedonia, former Yugoslav Republic of	MK
Madagascar	MG
Malawi	MW
Malaysia	MY
Maldives	MV
Mali	ML
Malta	MT
Mauritania	MR
Mauritius	MU
Mexico	MX
Monaco	MC
Mongolia	MN
Montserrat	MS
Morocco	MA
Mozambique	MZ
Myanmar	MM
Namibia	NA
Nauru	NR
Nepal	NP
Netherlands	NL
New Zealand	NZ
Nicaragua	NI
Niger	NE
Nigeria	NG
Norway	NO
Oman	OM
Pakistan	PK
Panama	PA
Papua New Guinea	PG
Paraguay	PY
Peru	PE
Philippines	PH
Poland	PL

Portugal	PT
Qatar	QA
Romania	RO
Russian Federation	RU
Rwanda	RW
St Helena	SH
St Kitts–Nevis	KN
St Lucia	LC
St Vincent and Grenadines	VC
Samoa	WS
San Marino	MS
Sao Tome and Principe	ST
Saudi Arabia	SA
Senegal	SN
Seychelles	SC
Sierra Leone	SL
Singapore	SG
Slovakia	SK
Slovenia	SI
Solomon Islands	SB
Somalia	SO
South Africa	ZA
Soviet Union, former	SU
Spain	ES
Sri Lanka	LK
Sudan	SD
Suriname	SR
Swaziland	SZ
Sweden	SE
Switzerland	CH
Syria	SY
Taiwan	TW
Tajikistan	TJ
Tanzania	TZ
Thailand	TH
Togo	TG
Tonga	TO
Trinidad and Tobago	TT
Tunisia	TN
Turkey	TR
Turkmenistan	TM
Turks and Caicos Islands	TC
Tuvalu	TV
Uganda	UG
Ukraine	UA
United Arab Emirates	AE

United Kingdom	GB
United States of America	US
Uruguay	UY
Uzbekistan	UZ
Vanuatu	VU
Vatican City State	VA
Venezuela	VE
Vietnam	VN
Western Sahara	EH
Yemen	YM
Yugoslavia	YU
Zambia	ZM
Zimbabwe	ZW

International organizations

ARIPO	AP
Benelux	BX
Eurasian Patent Convention	EA
European Patent Office	EP
Gulf Cooperation Council	GC
OAPI	OA
OHIM	EM
Patent Cooperation Treaty	WO

Codes used informally by Derwent Information for disclosure journals

Research Disclosures	RD
Technology Disclosures	TD

INDEX

Abstracts of patent specifications
European Patent Convention......24
Germany...............................65
Great Britain...........................38
Japan.......................................76
Patent Cooperation Treaty..........17
United States............................57

Bibliography
Basics of patent information.......10
Case law..................................120
Classification............................90
Current reviews........................121
Dictionaries and glossaries..........122
European Patent Convention......30,
112-13
Germany...............................70, 115
Great Britain.............................48,
112-13
Invention and patenting history..118
Japan...............................83, 116
Obtaining patent protection.......116
Patent Cooperation Treaty..........18
Patents as information................117
Statistics...................................121
United States............................60, 115

British Library...........................99
European Patent Convention......29
Germany...............................69
Great Britain.............................45
Japan.......................................81
Patent Cooperation Treaty..........17
United States............................59

Business method patents..........3

Case law
Bibliography.............................120
European Patent Convention.....29
Germany...............................69
Great Britain.............................43
Japan.......................................81
Searching.................................98
United States............................59

Classification
Bibliography.............................90
European Classification
(ECLA)....................................88
Great Britain classification..........89
International Patent
Classification............................85
Japanese classification................88
United States classification..........89

Country codes...........................129

Derwent Information
Classification............................89
World Patents Index..................110

Document codes........................5
European Patent Convention.....20
Germany...............................65
Great Britain.............................32
Japan.......................................71
Patent Cooperation Treaty..........13
United States............................49

European Patent Convention
Abstracts...................................24
Bibliography.............................30,
112-13
British Library...........................29
Case law...................................29
Gazettes...................................38
Great Britain.............................43
Internet databases.....................30
Numeration and document
codes.......................................20
Patenting procedure...................20
Search reports...........................22
Translations..............................29

Gazettes
European Patent Convention......24
Germany...............................65
Great Britain.............................38
Japan.......................................76
Patent Cooperation Treaty..........17
United States............................57

Germany
Abstracts....................................65
Bibliography........................70, 115
Case law.................................69
Gazette....................................65
Internet databases.....................70
Numeration and document
    codes..................................61
Patent Cooperation Treaty..........69
Patenting procedure 63
Search reports..........................65
Specifications...........................64
Utility models 63–5

Glossary.......................................124

Great Britain
Abstracts..................................38
Bibliography.............................48,
                    112–13
British Library..........................45
Case law.................................43
Classification 89
European Patent Convention......43
Internet databases.....................46
Numeration and document
    codes..................................32
Patent Cooperation Treaty..........40
Patent Office's information
    services................................44
Patenting procedure 32
Patents Information Network.....102
Search reports..........................36
Specifications...........................34

INID codes 127

Intellectual property.................1

Internet databases
see also Online
European Patent Convention......30
Germany..................................70
Great Britain 46
Japan 83
Patent Cooperation Treaty..........17
United States............................59

Japan
Abstracts..................................76
Bibliography.......................83, 116

British Library..........................81
Case law.................................81
Classifications 88
Gazette....................................76
Internet databases.....................83
Numeration and document
    codes..................................71
Patent Cooperation Treaty..........81
Patenting procedure 73
Search reports 76
Specifications 74
Utility models 72–3, 76

Licensing.....................................98

Microorganisms 4

Name searching 95

Numeration of patents
European Patent Convention......20
Germany..................................61
Great Britain 32
Japan 71
Patent Cooperation Treaty..........13
United States............................49

Online
databases................................107
hosts......................................106
resources 105
searching................................92

Patent Cooperation Treaty
Abstracts..................................17
Bibliography.............................18
British Library..........................17
Gazettes 17
Germany..................................69
Great Britain 40
Internet databases.....................17
Japan 81
Numeration and document
    codes..................................13
Patenting procedure 14
Search reports 15
Specifications 15
United States............................58

Patenting procedure 4
European Patent Convention 20

Germany..................................63
Great Britain...........................32
Japan....................................73
Patent Cooperation Treaty..........14
United States............................50

Patents
Advantages of...........................8
Criteria for granting..................2
Layout of specifications 7
Nature of................................2
Procedure for granting 4
Uses of..................................9

Patents Information Network..102

Pharmaceuticals.........................6

Search reports 8
European Patent Convention......22
Germany..................................65
Great Britain...........................36
Japan....................................76
Patent Cooperation Treaty..........15
United States............................56

Searching techniques.................92

Specifications 7
European Patent Convention......22
Germany..................................64
Great Britain...........................34

Japan....................................74
Patent Cooperation Treaty..........15
United States............................51

Status data................................96
European Patent Convention......24
Great Britain...........................46

**Supplementary Protection
Certificates**...............................6

United States
Abstracts..................................57
Bibliography............................60, 115
British Library..........................59
Case law..................................59
Classifications 89
Gazette...................................57
Internet sources........................59
Numeration and document
    codes..................................49
Other forms of patent
    documents............................58
Patent Cooperation Treaty..........58
Patenting procedure 50
Search reports..........................56
Specifications...........................51

Utility models...........................7
Germany..................................63-5
Japan....................................72-3, 76